Family Affairs

Family Affairs

Autorin: Ulrike Rudolph
Muttersprachliches Korrektorat:
Context Gesellschaft für Sprachen- und Mediendienste mbH
Satz: Noch & Noch
Covergestaltung: Marlies Müller
Coverillustration: Hauke Kock

Gesamtherstellung: Tandem Verlag GmbH

ISBN 978-3-8427-0641-5

www.tandem-verlag.de

Chapter 1

The girl's laughter is still ringing in the big car, as if she were still in it.

It is dark, not a single star is out. A thick layer[1] of clouds covers the sleeping town like a feather quilt. It is long after midnight. All youngsters should be in bed, safe and sound[2]. Even after a wild party to celebrate the beginning of the summer holidays.

Two shadows in long coats with a dog that looks like a black and white beer barrel[3] on a leash[4] can hardly manage to jump from the street onto the walkway in an effort to escape the rushing car. They save their lives, and the fat dog's. He growls[5] accusingly[6]. The dog owners look at each other in the milky light of a street lamp. They shake their heads in anger.

"Irresponsible[7]! Absolutely irresponsible! The driver must be insane[8]! He could have killed Hamlet!", shrieks the old man and crumbles his rain hat between his hands.

The white haired lady bends down to the barrel-like dog and pats his head.

"Are you okay, my little sweetheart?"

"Bastards! Did you hear the volume of the music? One should report that car to the police!"

The man shakes his fist behind the car, but it has long vanished[9], around the corner of the village hall, in the direction of the river.

"Let's do that, Honey! Call the police right away. Have you got the plate number[10], Richard?"

1 layer – Schicht 2 safe and sound – gesund und munter 3 beer barrel – Bierfass 4 leash – Leine 5 to growl – knurren 6 accusing – anklagend, vorwurfsvoll 7 irresponsible – unverantwortlich 8 insane – verrückt, wahnsinnig 9 to vanish – verschwinden 10 plate number – Nummernschild

The woman looks at her husband with a visible doubt in her face. He puts up his hat again and frowns[11].

Exercise 1

Wessen? Setze die folgenden Begriffe in den Genitiv.

1. *the car + number plate* the car's number plate
2. *The man + hat* the man's hat
3. *the woman + dog* the woman's dog

"It was too quick, Heather. Really, when I looked up from Hamlet it was too far away."

The old lady shakes her head, but she smiles.

"As always, Richard, too slow! Not only don't we sleep well, we are getting slow…"

"Come on, Heather, we are not getting old. That car was quick as a rocket! And I would not wonder if we read about a speeding accident[12] in tomorrow's paper."

The car crosses the bridge, without any respect for the lovely old buildings at its side and the beauty of the place. It races towards the next village south of Bath. The music is cranked up[13] to full volume. The hard rhythm of an old Metallica song hammers out of the speakers and makes even the high-quality doors of the new SUV tremble[14]. The vibrations mix with the still fresh memory of the laughter and the dance floor music from the party.

11 to frown – die Stirn runzeln 12 speeding accident – Unfall wegen überhöhter Geschwindigkeit 13 to crank up – aufdrehen 14 to tremble – zittern

Exercise 2

Zeitreise: Setze die folgenden Verben ins Präsens.

1. *The dog (barked)* the dog barks
2. *The man (frowned)* the man frowns
3. *The lady (shook)* the lady shakes *her head.*

The red streetlights mean nothing. The car almost flies towards its destination.

As the car hits the high kerbstone[15], where the broad city street meets the narrow country road, it starts to skid[16]. Two wheels are in the air. A screeching[17] of metal on stone cuts through the night, a symphony of energy, freedom and destruction. Somehow the car does not turn over[18], it drops down to the road again, finds some grip on the old cobble stone pavement and rushes on.

At a sharp left turn in the countryside, where some post boxes and three green and blue dustbins indicate that a house is hidden behind the huge hedges, the car knocks down the dustbins, but it evades the post-boxes.

This time the car starts skidding severely[19]. It turns around in a circle in the middle of the road and glides down a dip[20] which is wet from last day's rain. The car hits the green hedge on the right with its rear[21]. There must be a wall hidden under the green plants. The ugly[22] noise outside is even louder than the hammering music inside the car. But it does not come to a stop, it turns

15 kerbstone – Bordstein 16 to skid – schleudern 17 to screech – kreischen 18 to turn over – umkippen 19 severe – ernsthaft 20 dip – Abhang 21 rear – Heck 22 ugly – hässlich

again, scratches along the wall with its side and finally bumps[23] into an old beech tree[24] on the right hand side of the road.

Exercise 3

Parallelwelten: Finde die Gegenteilpaare und verbinde sie mit Strichen.

loud	*bright*
dark	*cold*
fat	*silent*
day	*slim*
hot	*night*

23 to bump – prallen 24 beech tree – Buche

Chapter 2

"What is wrong with you, young lady?"

Linda turns her face away from her mother, who is looking backwards from the passenger's[1] seat.

Outside green hills are rushing by. The sun is out and only a few white clouds linger over the huge rocks which form Stonehenge, an ancient place of worship or whatever. Linda cannot remember what they learned about it at school and she does not care at all.

Old rocks, that's all.

Her head feels like one of them, or at least as if one had fallen on her last night.

Why does her mother have to be so caring? Why can't she just leave her alone for a while?

Linda shakes her head.

"And by the way, what is that dark spot on your neck? It looks like a love bite[2]!!!!"

Linda feels for the dot with her hand. This morning she could hardly recognize herself in the mirror, otherwise she would have covered the mark[3] with a scarf[4]. Her mother can be as annoying as Jamie, her little brother.

Her mother has not yet finished: "Did you drink Rattler[5] again? Don't you know that you are far too young for alcohol? How it damages your brain?"

Linda has not got the power to answer these questions.

"Come on, Eileen," her father says instead.

He smiles at Linda through the driver's mirror.

1 passenger – Beifahrer 2 love bite – Knutschfleck 3 mark – *hier:* Fleck 4 scarf – Schal 5 Rattler – Apfelwein

"Remember how you liked cider at her age. Just give our daughter a painkiller[6] and she'll never drink again and soon be texting[7] her friends again."

"Oh Matthew, you are so …"

Exercise 4

Zeitreise: Setze die Verben in die einfache Vergangenheit (*past tense*, z. B. *went*).

1. *Her head (feels)* felt *like a stone.*
2. *Linda (shakes)* shook *her head.*
3. *Her mother (is)* was *annoying.*

Her mother turns her head to her husband. Her voice is shrill. Linda relaxes. As long as these two are talking with each other, she is okay. She just does not want to argue[8]. Not about the party last night, not about her condition and not by any means[9] about her relationship with Cooper. But a painkiller would really be a brilliant idea. She had had several Peach Rattlers, five or six at least[10]. They had fun, that's for sure. And a bit of distress[11], because Linda had to leave for damned Cornwall and Cooper had to stay in Bath, without her.

Rattler is a strong cider, stronger than the beer the guys had. Maybe she had one too many. Linda can hardly remember how she got home. Did Cooper take her home? Did her father come to get her? Or did she walk?

6 painkiller – Schmerztablette 7 to text – *hier:* SMS schreiben 8 to argue – sich streiten, diskutieren 9 not by any means – auf gar keinen Fall 10 at least – mindestens 11 distress – Leid, Kummer

Exercise 5

Vieles: Bilde den Plural der folgenden Substantive!

1. *woman* women
2. *dog* dogs
3. *man* men
4. *child* children
5. *house* houses

Cooper must have accompanied[12] her home, that's what he usually does. And she must have been at home in time[13], by midnight. If not, her mother would have complained about that, too. And she would have grounded[14] Linda for one or two weeks.

Who cares about being grounded in Cornwall? Linda thinks. What would the highlights be there at night?

Exercise 6

Besserwisser: Was ist in den folgenden Sätzen richtig, Adjektiv (z. B. *light, good*) oder Adverb (z. B. *lightly, well*)? Setze die richtige Form ein.

1. *(Loud)* Loud *music came from the car.*
2. *The car drove (quick)* quickly
3. *The old man watched the car (careful)* carefully

12 to accompany – begleiten 13 in time – rechtzeitig 14 to ground – Hausarrest erteilen

A folk singer in the pub? A round of Bingo in the town hall? A long walk along the harbour, preferably[15] hand in hand with her little brother?

Linda looks to the left of the back seat.

Jamie is sitting in a relaxed way, his head resting on the headrest[16], both eyes closed, his hair hanging in shiny streaks[17] like liquid fudge into his face. He has been fast asleep since they got on the motorway, humming[18] as he often does when he feels safe and comfortable. Not even the roundabouts wake him up, although his head drops to the side and back. But he is not sleeping deep enough to let the rabbit skeleton go[19]. His love for all kinds of bones and skeletons is one of the many freakish whims[20] he has been driving Linda crazy[21] with since the first day of his life, twelve years ago.

Exercise 7

Satzsalat: Bringe die Wörter in die richtige Reihenfolge!

1. *a strong is Rattler cider.*

   Rattler is a strong cider

2. *have must her home accompanied Cooper.*

   Cooper must have accompanied her home

3. *motorway has asleep Jamie been they got on deep since the.*

   Jamie has been deep asleep since got on the motorway

15 preferably – am besten 16 headrest – Kopfstütze 17 streak – Strähne 18 to hum – brummen 19 to let go – loslassen 20 whim – Marotte 21 to drive crazy – wahnsinnig machen

Even at nights, in his dreams, Jamie does not stop counting most of the time. At home their parents sometimes laugh about his habits[22]. As long as there is a door they can close between him and them every once in a while.

Maybe their parents gave him sleeping syrup to keep him from counting, to at least have a silent journey?

Linda has often thought about how to calm Jamie down, stop him from counting everything countable or from arranging words in alphabetical order, another spleen[23].

Nevertheless, he is her little brother and she has to care for him. Even if that is not easy all the time.

„This holiday will solve many problems. It will … bring us closer together as a family," she had heard her father whisper[24] to her mother after they had booked the apartment in St Ives several weeks ago. Which was and is a major catastrophe for her and Cooper. They need each other so very much.

Oh, Cooper. I will text you as soon as I can!

Exercise 8

Zeitreise: Setze die Verben ins Perfekt (*present perfect*, z. B. *has gone*).

1. *Jamie (falls) ________________ asleep in the car.*
2. *Linda (is) has been ________________ fed up with the holidays.*
3. *Their parents (are) ________________ happy.*

22 habit – Gewohnheit 23 spleen – Tick 24 to whisper – flüstern

Linda knows perfectly well that it is her behaviour towards Jamie, but also the whole thing with him, the school problems, the lack of friends, her mother's bad feelings about social networks in general and about Linda's internet activities in particular[25]. And that her father has almost been a stranger to them because he has been working a lot of overtime since the company fired some of his colleagues. All these subjects are the reasons for this holiday, and she will have to show some concern if she wants to get a bit of freedom for herself and maybe for Cooper over the next two weeks.

While she looks at Jamie, who makes funny movements with his nose as if he is dreaming of nice smells, her mobile phone starts ringing. Her mother turns her head.

Linda shrugs her shoulders[26] and says: "I'll keep it short." Then she answers the call: "Yes?"

It is Ruby, her best friend and Cooper's sister.

Ruby says: "Where are you now?"

Exercise 9

Besserwisser: Steigere die folgenden Adjektive.

1. *loud,* ________________, ________________
2. *good,* ________________, ________________
3. *short,* ________________, ________________
4. *careful,* ________________, ________________
5. *nice,* ________________, ________________

25 in particular – im Besonderen 26 to shrug one's shoulders – mit den Schultern zucken

As Linda's mother's face grows angry Linda says: "In the car. Can't speak at the moment. Let's talk after we arrive, okay?"

Without waiting for Ruby to answer Linda hangs up.

"I know, I know …," she says and her mother nods and turns around.

During this holiday, each member of the family has a subject to deal with. Hers is, according to[27] her mother's judgment[28], avoiding[29] media for social contacts. The use of her mobile phone should be restricted to absolutely necessary messages. Facebook and Student's Network are to be avoided at all cost.

She is only allowed to use the mobile for vitally[30] important messages only, like: "I'm dying[31]! Dying of boredom in this car!"

27 according to – entsprechend, gemäß 28 judgement – Beurteilung, Urteilsspruch 29 to avoid – meiden 30 vital – lebenswichtig 31 to die – sterben

Chapter 3

"Come on, Linda, let's go! Let's face the last 100 Miles!"

Linda can hear her father, but she can't see him. He is behind the shelf with crisps and cookies in the petrol station[1], together with her mother.

Linda has taken the chance offered by her parents and brother going to the toilet to walk into the station and take out her mobile to inform Cooper that she is having a really hard time as texting is almost impossible.

Linda finishes her message:

"Can't text. Parents. Get back at night. Love"

Then she closes her mobile and puts it in her bag.

Her father is looking at her over the rack. She has to respond. "Can I get a Diet Coke, please?"

It's her mother, who replies.

"Just take a lemonade, love, that's better for you."

Her mother takes a can from the shelf and hands it over to her husband who is already queuing[2] in front of the cash counter[3].

Her mother puts an arm around Linda's shoulders.

"It's going to be great, believe me. St Ives is the most beautiful place in Cornwall. Five beaches! And our apartment is right at the biggest of them, the surf place. That's cool! If you like, you can take a course."

They are crossing the car park in front of the service station.

"I haven't got a wet suit," Linda replies.

What a stupid idea: Her on a surf board, in one of those tight black

1 petrol station – Tankstelle 2 to queue – Schlange stehen 3 cash counter – Kassentresen

suits which make everybody look like a dancing liver sausage. Everybody, apart from Cooper. He would look quite nice in one of those.

"I am surely not going into that icy water!"

Exercise 10

Wortverdreher: Bilde Fragen aus den folgenden Sätzen, indem du die Wortstellung veränderst und – wo nötig – Wörter ergänzt.

1. *Jamie counts everything.*

   ____

2. *Linda wants to be with Cooper.*

   ____

3. *Their mother is suggesting solutions.*

   ____

Linda opens the back door of the car and sits down. Her mother is already in the car. As her father starts the engine, his hand suddenly freezes, the motor stays quiet.

"Aren't we missing somebody?"

Her mother turns around and gets pale.

Not really, is Linda's first thought as she realises her little brother is missing.

"I'll go and get him," she says instead and starts running towards the toilets.

Chapter 4

… 4,223, 4,224, 4,225, 4,226, 4,227, 4,228, 4,229, 4,230 …

Hmmm …

Black, blue, dark grey, green, grey, light blue, red, silver, white, yellow …

Hmmm …

4,231, 4,232, 4,233, 4,234, 4,235, 4,236, 4,237, 4,238, 4,239, 4,240 …

Exercise 11

Zeitreise: Setze die Verben in die Zukunftsform (*future*, z. B. *will go*).

1. *Jamie (is collecting) ________________ colours.*
2. *Linda (looks) ________________ for him.*
3. *Their father (sends) ________________ Linda after Jamie.*

Hmmm …

Rabbit skeleton: atlas[1], cervical vertebrae[2] …

1 atlas – Atlaswirbel 2 cervical vertebra - Halswirbel

Bolt[3]!

Bolt! Bolt! Bolt! Bolt!

C-V-C – Wrong! Wrong! Wrong!

Vertebrae!!

Does "vertebrae" belong here? Or nearer the end of the alphabet? Between u and w? To be precise between vers … and veru…?

Bolt! Bolt! Bolt! Bolt!

It is hard to breathe!

It is hot!

What shall I do?

Shall I split "cervical vertebrae" into two? May that be done? Would that still be correct?

Or shall I go on: cervical vertebrae, cranium[4], mandible[5], scapula[6] …?

As if nothing had happened?

That would only be correct if cervical vertebrae could be taken as one word. But it is two.

What am I to do to keep up the order?

Bolt! Bolt! Bolt! Bolt! Bolt!

The air is thin in here!

I can hardly breathe!

I have to slap[7] my chest[8]!

3 bolt – Blitz, Bolzen 4 cranium – Hirnschädel 5 mandible – Unterkiefer 6 scapula – Schulterblatt 7 to slap – gegen etwas schlagen 8 chest – Brustkorb

This is what I have to do!
Something is wrong!
Vertebrae is in the wrong place!
It is disturbing the whole order!

Exercise 12

Buchstabensalat: Sortiere die Buchstaben so, dass sinnvolle Wörter entstehen!

1. *ingeen* ____________________
2. *mesodybo* ____________________
3. *otitle* ____________________

4,240, 4,243, 4,142, 3,542 …

It does not work!

Bolt! Bolt! Bolt! Bolt!

Chapter 5

As Linda enters the men's toilets, she is in panic about her brother and does not care if a man might be irritated about a lady's visit to this very private place. Fortunately there is no one there.

Jamie stands all alone in the middle of the washroom like a statue, eyes wide open, but mentally[1] far away. He looks as if he sees something horrible in the far distance, something he cannot reach. This might be the reason why he hits himself with his fists like mad, saying "bolt, bolt, bolt" again and again. Maybe he imagines bolts hitting himself. Linda never knows. Nobody does.

What she knows at once is that something really bad must have happened to her little brother's strange sense of order in this place. Maybe he thought some invisible rays from the toilet flushes[2] or the hand dryers had hit him, maybe he had to stop counting because somebody walked into his sight, blocking him from his desired counting objects. Here it could have been the tiles[3] on the walls.

Whatever it was, she must stop him hitting himself.

The only thing that will calm him down at once will be a new stimulus, something he can count or arrange, like a set of bones he can put into the right order. But, unfortunately, she has no dead animal at hand.

Linda looks around while she tries to get Jamie's attention, but he still looks through her.

Linda speaks in a low and consoling voice to him, telling him everything that comes into her mind, about the holidays, about

1 mentally – geistig 2 toilet flush – Toilettenspülung 3 tile – Fliese

his rabbit skeleton, as her mother has advised her. She does this although she is convinced that she cannot reach him right now. Her mother always thinks it works.

Exercise 13

Lückenfüller: Setze die richtigen Präpositionen ein.

1. *Linda is in panic ____________ her brother.*
2. *Jamie likes to put bones ____________ the right order.*
3. *Somebody might have walked ____________ his sight.*

Jamie goes on hitting himself as if Linda were not by his side, as if she did not exist at all. He needs help, preferably from Doc Wiseguy, his psychiatrist[4], who seems to know her brother best.

Where is the little notebook Doc Wiseguy gave him? The images of faces in that book help Jamie find out what people's intentions are, what they want from him. Her mother always fixes it to Jamie's belt in the morning.

Linda lifts her brother's wide blue T-shirt and gets some of his punches against her arms. All of Jamie's clothes have to be at least one size too big and this special sort of sea blue. He doesn't accept other clothes.

There is a big bruise[5] on his belly, the size of a grapefruit, right above his belly button[6]. Linda frowns. This cannot be from hitting himself. Can it? No. Usually he doesn't really hurt himself that badly. And the bruise must definitely be older. Has he had

4 psychiatrist – Psychiater 5 bruise – Bluterguss 6 belly button – Bauchnabel

one of those attacks[7] the day before? Only stronger than usual? No. Her mother would have told her. So where did Jamie get this injury? Anyway, right now he is hitting himself!

There is the notebook. Dangling down from the blue belt that keeps Jamie's shorts in their place.

Linda grabs it and quickly turns the plastic covered cardboard pages with faces and gestures until she finds the figure with a raised hand, showing the index finger. The typical teacher's gesture telling the kids to be quiet and listen well.

Exercise 14

Hauptsache: Unterstreiche die Substantive (keine Namen!) im vorigen Absatz und setze sie in den Plural oder Singular.

____

____

____

She lifts the picture in front of Jamie's eyes and moves it around there, trying to get his attention. Some seconds later he reacts and focuses on the picture.

That's good.

His hitting slows down, and he starts to put breaks[8] between his "bolts".

Now she needs something for him to do. Instantly, or she will lose him again.

7 attack – Anfall 8 break – Pause

Exercise 15

Strippenzieher: Verbinde die folgenden *phrasal verbs* (Verb mit Partikel) mit der richtigen deutschen Übersetzung.

to go off	*anstreben*
to go for	*sich freuen auf*
to look for	*explodieren*
to look forward to	*suchen*

As she is looking around she has the idea. It might work.

She runs into one of the toilet cubicles[9] and takes the paper roll from its hook. She rushes back to Jamie, smiling. He has stopped hitting himself and stands in complete silence.

Her eyes catch his. Linda starts pulling leaves[10] from the paper roll and hands them to Jamie. Leaf by leaf. She counts "one, two, three …"

Jamie watches her hands and takes the sheets of toilet paper in his as if he were receiving presents or pieces of treasure[11].

Finally he calms down and follows Linda to the car.

9 cubicle – Kabine 10 leaf – Blatt 11 treasure – Schatz

Chapter 6

It is late in the afternoon. Clouds have collected over Bath. The town and the surrounding villages have lost their summer appearance. The limestone buildings and the Abbey have almost lost their bright colours. The river flows in silence in a heavy and dirty green. The trees by the roads leading out of the town centre look like the huge shadows of some muddy giants. Even the pink hydrangea[1] in the garden of Ruby and Cooper's parental home[2] look colourless and somehow depressive.

Ruby puts down the grey rubbish bag, turns away from the open terrace doors and lets herself fall into one of the three white leather sofas. She turns towards her brother.

"Let's take a break. Time enough. They'll only be back the day after tomorrow."

Cooper sets down the ashtray[3] he was just cleaning at the marble[4] table and moans as he sinks into one of the other sofas.

"I'm not sure we'll get the cigarette stink out in time."

He holds his belly.

Obviously he had a few beers too many last night.

Ruby thinks a stomach ache[5] is exactly what her brother has earned. It was not okay that he left the party together with Melinda, one of his class mates, long after Linda had left. She is not quite sure if she should question him about his motives for that. They are so obvious.

On the other hand Ruby had several Rattlers with Linda, too, and some more after Linda had left. There is a funny mixture of

1 hydrangea – Hortensie 2 parental home – Elternhaus 3 ashtray – Aschenbecher 4 marble – Marmor 5 stomach ache – Bauchschmerzen

pictures in Ruby's head, and she is not sure if all of them are real or if imagination and dreams are involved.

Exercise 16

Besserwisser: Welche der folgenden Aussagen ist falsch?

1. *Linda is looking forward to their holiday in Cornwall.*
2. *Jamie likes wearing blue clothes.*
3. *Cooper is Ruby's brother.*

The strange thing about what she remembers is Jamie, Linda's little brother, appearing late at night at the far end of the garden. It is not his appearance, what worries her. It wouldn't have been the first time that Jamie had followed Linda, just to watch what she was doing. What really worries Ruby is the fact that she cannot connect Jamie's appearance with an exact point in time. She does not know if it was before or after Linda had left.

Right now Cooper is hanging on the sofa like a wet towel. He rubs his head. He has a headache too.

She hears herself again calling Jamie last night, but he didn't come forward to her, as he quite often does, but disappeared. And when she looked where he had gone, she discovered him in the garage, behind the steering wheel of her father's brand new car. Windscreen wipers[6] on, which would have been very much like Jamie, who likes all kinds of visible repetitions[7].

6 windscreen wiper – Scheibenwischer 7 repetition – Wiederholung

Exercise 17

Lückenfüller: Ergänze das fehlende Wort!

1. *Ruby puts down the grey ________________ bag.*
2. *Ruby thinks a ________________ is exactly what her brother has earned.*
3. *She cannot connect Jamie's ________________ with an exact point in time.*

Had she gone in and pulled Jamie out of the car because she feared her father might find out about a visitor there? He might be more likely to[8] realise somebody had been in his car than in the house. Or had she called Linda to come and take care of her little brother?

Ruby closes her eyes and tries to concentrate. But the only thing she can feel clearly is the beating of her heart in both of her temples[9]. It feels as if a drum is hitting her from the inside of her poor brain.

Has she really seen Jamie? Or was it a dream? Like Cooper leaving with Melinda? Everything is kind of grey and blurred[10] today.

Ruby decides, not to ask Cooper about Melinda. He is looking bad enough already. And they still have to clear the whole house of the traces[11] the party has left. And fill the fridge up again and the freezer as well.

8 be more likely to – *hier:* eher 9 temple – Schläfe 10 blurred – verschwommen 11 traces – Spuren

Exercise 18

Verbbeuger: Ergänze die fehlenden Konjugationsformen der folgenden Verben (z. B. *go, went, gone*).

1. *hear,* ____________________, ____________________
2. *look,* ____________________, ____________________
3. *see,* ____________________, ____________________

Their parents will come back in two days time, and if they find out about the party, which they had definitely forbidden, they will give Ruby and Cooper a hard time over the holidays.

Ruby sighs[12] deeply and leans forward to pick up a piece of pizza, which is stuck[13] on the carpet like chewing gum.

Cooper coughs like their grandfather. Obviously he is still worried about the cigarette smoke. Then he clears his throat as if he wants to give a speech.

Ruby looks up from the damaged[14] carpet.

Her brother shuffles his feet around[15] on the floor and watches his own movements as if they were the most important thing in the world.

Ruby knows her brother too well. He is about to make an important statement. At least important for himself.

Ruby sits up straight, watching Cooper.

Finally he stops shuffling his feet and looks at her.

"I've got to tell you something important."

12 to sigh – seufzen 13 to stick – festkleben 14 damaged – beschädigt 15 to shuffle around – herumschieben

Exercise 19

Fundstücke: Finde am Anfang des Kapitels die englischen Entsprechungen zu diesen Sätzen und unterstreiche sie oder schreibe sie auf die Linien.

1. *Offenbar hat er letzte Nacht ein paar Bier zu viel gehabt.*
2. *Wieder hört sie sich in der letzten Nacht nach Jamie rufen.*
3. *Ruby beschließt, Cooper nicht nach Melinda zu fragen.*

1. ____

2. ____

3. ____

Chapter 7

Back in the car Jamie is busy arranging the pieces of toilet paper on the tray[1] he always needs to keep working on, to put the bones of some remainder[2] of a meal together like the rabbit skeleton, his latest piece of art[3]. Now he is arranging the sheets so they lay in a circle, covering each other like fish scales[4]. This has kept him busy for the last hour.

Their father is turning into the Harbour Road of St Ives.

"Look, how nice"! Her mother exclaims.

Linda looks around. The sun is out, only a few white clouds are hanging over the sea.

Well.

There is a crowded road with restaurants and shops to the left, hundreds of pedestrians[5] in the street and on the walkway to their right. Behind them a small harbour, which has fallen dry with low tide[6]. A handful of fishing boats are lying on the beach, dropped to one side. Only the dry part of the harbour, close to the road, looks bright, it is obviously sand. Some kids are playing there. Maybe that's the beach. The wetter parts are covered with algae[7] or seaweed[8]. A strong smell of salt, fish and perhaps the wet sea plants is lingering[9] over the street and coming in through the open car window. What is most remarkable is a screeching sound that tortures[10] Linda's ears and brings back the horrible headache she thought she had lost after the drink.

1 tray – Tablett 2 remainder – Rest 3 piece of art – Kunstwerk 4 fish scale – Fischschuppe 5 pedestrians – Fußgänger 6 low tide – Ebbe 7 algae – Algen 8 seaweed – Seetang 9 to linger – sich aufhalten, schweben 10 to torture – foltern

Exercise 20

Lückenfüller: Häng das passende Frageanhängsel (*question tag*, z. B. *You haven't seen her, have you?*) an.

1. *Ruby saw Jamie in the car, ________________?*
2. *Linda hasn't taken her mobile out, ________________?*
3. *Jamie counted the tiles, ________________?*

"Seagulls," she states[11] as she watches one of the birds steal a cone[12] of ice-cream from a man. He ducks[13] his head under the beat of the bird's wings.

Those seagulls are the size of shoeboxes. Linda cannot remember having seen so many of such big birds before. They are everywhere: up in the air, sitting on the handrails[14] around the harbour, prancing[15] over the beach. Waiting and watching out for somebody unaware of their attention to his food.

Exercise 21

Just do it: Unterstreiche die Verben im vorigen Absatz und konjugiere sie durch.

____

____

____

11 to state – feststellen 12 cone – Hörnchen 13 to duck – in Deckung gehen 14 handrail – Geländer
15 to prance – stolzieren

By her side, Jamie stops arranging the pieces of toilet paper. He looks at the seagulls.

"I like those birds," he says and starts counting.

Linda turns her head, looking out for the open sea and the promised beaches. At the far end of a pier, which almost circles the harbour, is a small lighthouse. At its side she sees an opening to the sea. And in the distance, shining in the sun like a diamond in all that blue, there is a tiny elevation[16], green like young snow peas[17] with a sparkling white tower on top.

"Godrevy Lighthouse," her mother whispers full of awe[18]. "Virginia Woolfe took it as inspiration for her novel 'To The Lighthouse'. You two will come to that at school one day."

"You bet[19]," Linda replies, as her mother turns around to see her reaction. "But where are the beaches?"

Exercise 22

Was wäre, wenn: Ergänze die fehlenden Verbformen in den folgenden If-Sätzen (Typ 1).

1. *If the sun shines, they (go)* ________________ *swimming.*
2. *If they arrive in time, Linda (call)* ________________ *Cooper.*
3. *If the apartment is too small, she (go)* ________________ *crazy.*

"Just a minute," her father says as he enters one of the narrow roads leading into the old town. Small white two-storey[20] houses

16 elevation – Erhebung 17 snow pea – Zuckererbse 18 awe – Ehrfurcht 19 you bet – aber sicher! 20 two-storey – zweigeschossig

with blue and green wooden doors and windows frame the road. Another car has to move backwards to let them pass. There is not the space for two of them.

As he loses sight of the seagulls, Jamie starts complaining: "I like those birds!"

Linda lifts a piece of paper and Jamie turns his attention back to that and seems okay.

When their father turns the car into the open gate of a huge apartment building, Linda's phone rings again.

CHAPTER 8

The view from the kitchen is fabulous[1]. A gigantic sandy beach, bordered[2] by a nice little peninsula[3] with a natural stone chapel on top. To the left of the beach, in the far distance, the green coastal path starts right behind a funny white, round building with a lot of glass at the front and some older houses. The cliffs below the path build a natural border for the surfers who keep the second half of the beach under their control.

EXERCISE 23

„Am Lesen sein": Setze die folgenden Verben in die Verlaufsform.

1. *Jamie (counts) ________________ tiles.*
2. *Linda (reads) ________________ a book.*
3. *Their father (drives) ________________ the car.*

The flat[4] itself seems to be okay, too. Linda will have a room for herself, as Jamie gets a small room next to her parents' bedroom.

This might open up the opportunity of leaving the flat at night, if … well, if Linda can manage to just talk or text with Cooper, if her Mum gives her a break[5]. Which seems most unlikely[6] at the moment. She is still angry because of Cooper's last attempt to talk to Linda a few minutes ago. Although Linda had just rejected[7] the call.

1 fabulous – fabelhaft 2 Border – begrenzen 3 peninsula – Halbinsel 4 flat – Wohnung 5 to give s.o. a break – jmdm. eine Pause geben 6 unlikely – unwahrscheinlich 7 to reject – abweisen

Exercise 24

Zukunftsmusik: Bilde die Zukunftsform, die eine feste Absicht ausdrückt oder unmittelbar bevorsteht (mit *going to*).

1. *Linda (call) ________________ Ruby.*
2. *Her Dad (lock) ________________ the car.*
3. *Her Mum (cook) ________________ dinner.*

Her father is out of breath just like herself and Jamie. On their way back to the garage to get the last remaining bags from the car, a tall man with the face of an old horse stops them at the top of the open staircase.

"Hi, you guys! Great to meet you."

"And you," says Linda's father.

"I'm Paul Bannister, Minneapolis. United States. Just arrived two days ago. With my daughter Debby."

Exercise 25

Was wäre, wenn: Ergänze die fehlenden Verbformen in den folgenden If-Sätzen (Typ 2).

1. *If Jamie was cool, he (feel) ______________ better.*
2. *If their Mum cooked good food, they (eat) ____________ at home.*
3. *If Linda drank Rattler, she (get) ______________ drunk.*

The man is about her father's age with a haircut like an American college boy of twenty, khaki coloured shorts and white socks and trainers. He turns around and shouts for his daughter. He goes on talking.

As a girl about Linda's age[8] comes out of the neighbouring apartment, Linda knows at once that she is a teacher's pet[9]: shiny blonde, cute[10] shoulder-length hair, blue eyes, flouncy[11] blouse, skirt. Most certainly[12] she plays the recorder[13] and sings in the school choir. Only her prominent[14] angular[15] chin indicates that she might not only be nice but has a will of her own, a strong will, if she is like Cooper's classmate Melinda, who has the same kind of chin.

"Hi there."

Exercise 26

Können und dürfen: Übersetze die folgenden Sätze und verwende *to be able to* oder *to be allowed to.*

1. *Jamie kann zählen.*

   ____

2. *Linda kann nicht telefonieren.*

   ____

3. *Sie kann auch keine SMS schicken.*

   ____

8 about o.'s age – ungefähr im gleichen Alter 9 teacher's pet – Streberin 10 cute – niedlich 11 flouncy – rüschenbesetzt 12 most certainly – ganz bestimmt 13 recorder – Blockflöte 14 prominent – vorstehend 15 angular – eckig

Paul Bannister tells them about Debby visiting the Tate Gallery for a course in painting and how nice it would be if Jamie and Linda joined her the next day. He somehow manages to get Jamie's attention. Maybe it's the pattern of his shirt, which is plaid[16] like a tartan[17] in red and green, maybe it's the sound of his voice. You never know what attracts Jamie. But her brother behaves quite normally and nods as if he likes the idea.

As her mother joins into the conversation about what's on in St Ives, Linda imagines herself following Debby and Jamie to the Tate Gallery the next morning to take part in some funny painting or drawing course. Or maybe a course in playing the recorder, if the offering at the Tate is as wide as Paul Bannister tells them.

Exercise 27

Müssen: Setze die korrekte Form von *must* oder *have to* in den folgenden Sätzen ein.

1. *You __________________ eat that.*
2. *Linda __________________ put her mobile phone away.*
3. *Their father __________________ lock the door.*

Linda walks down the stairs to get the last bag and after that unpacks her stuff. As long as their parents are involved in talking she might, at last, get the opportunity to answer Cooper's call.

16 plaid – kariert 17 tartan – Schottenstoff

Chapter 9

Ruby watches Cooper turn pale. He was totally mistaken when he took up the telephone receiver pleasantly anticipating[1] talking to Linda.

It's their parents. And obviously they are coming back one day earlier than expected!

Gosh! They have not yet finished cleaning the house and they still have to go shopping!

Exercise 28

Nicht müssen: Bilde die Verneinung der folgenden Sätze.

1. *You must eat that.*

   ____

2. *Linda must put her mobile phone away.*

   ____

3. *Their father must lock the door.*

   ____

As Cooper tells her, right after the fact that their parents had changed their plans, his important news is that he is going to

1 to anticipate – erwarten, erhoffen

follow Linda to Cornwall, no discussion, she doesn't know what to say.

Obviously the vision of Cooper leaving with Melinda had been a bad dream and he is really in love with Linda.

And why shouldn't he go?

Exercise 29

Nicht dürfen: Übersetze die folgenden Sätze.

1. *Linda darf das Handy nicht benutzen.*

   ____

2. *Jamie darf nicht alleine rausgehen.*

   ____

3. *Ihre Eltern dürfen nicht streiten.*

   ____

Their parents would accept his leaving. They had given up telling Cooper what to do a year ago. Her brother has done what he wanted since he had turned 16, no matter what his family thought about his plans. These are the summer holidays and Cooper had saved the money he earned in the last holidays. So why shouldn't he go?

And why does she feel so bad about him leaving? Is it because he doesn't want to wait until their parents are back? Is it because he wants her to tell them he is with his friend Franklin, who has travelled to Scotland with his parents? His explanation, that Linda's parents don't know he is coming, should be enough to justify a lie. But why doesn't he tell this lie himself, but instead gets Ruby involved in it?

"Well, let's hurry up to get the fridge filled up again," he says and claps his hands. "Let's go right now, we can finish the cleaning later on. I want everything to be spick and span[2] before I go. Don't want to leave my little sister in a mess."

"Okay," Ruby replies. "Then let's take the bikes to get all that stuff together. Do you remember what we had in the fridge before the party?"

Exercise 30

Fundstücke: Finde im Anfang des Kapitels die englischen Entsprechungen zu diesen Sätzen und unterstreiche sie.

1. *Ihre Eltern würden akzeptieren, dass er abgehauen ist.*
2. *Und warum fühlt sie sich wegen seines Abhauens so schlecht?*
3. *Ruby beobachtet, wie Cooper blass wird.*

Cooper scratches his forehead.

"Yes, I do know. It's all in here! A full shopping list!"

As they leave the house and Ruby turns to the garage for the bikes he stops her.

"Let's walk."

2 spick and span – blitzblank

"But the bags will be too heavy to carry them."

"Let's walk. We can't talk on the bikes. I'll carry the bags."

Ruby agrees. It is unusual enough that her big brother is joining her as she goes shopping.

"So why don't you tell Mum and Dad where you are going?"

Exercise 31

Wessen? Setze die folgenden Begriffe in den Genitiv.

1. *Ruby + vision* ______________________
2. *Their parents + house* ______________________
3. *Ruby and Cooper + parents* ______________________

"Because I don't know where I will stay. You know, Linda's parents don't expect me there. And as Linda might have told you, they are under a kind of relationship stress. Her father works too much, her mother wants everybody to take over more responsibility for Jamie. She is full of sorrow about him and his future. And she especially wants Linda to care more for Jamie. The holiday is apparently some sort of test for her. Now can you imagine what they will say when Dad calls? Telling them I'm joining in?"

"They'll freak out[3]," Ruby says.

"Exactly. That's why I want you to tell them about Scotland. But if you don't like the idea, I can write and leave them a letter.

3 to freak out – ausrasten

Do you remember Dad complaining about the dead spots[4] when he was on this business trip in Edinburgh last May? That will keep them from trying to get me on the phone."

"Quite clever," Ruby says. "But where will you stay in reality, if Linda's parents don't know you are there? I mean, what chances do you have of meeting Linda anyhow?"

Exercise 32

Zeitreise: Setze die folgenden Verben ins Präsens.

1. *Ruby (heard) ________________ Cooper talk on the phone.*
2. *The car (drove) ________________ too fast.*
3. *Their parents (came) ________________ home early.*

Cooper drags Ruby away from the direction of the local grocery store.

"Where are we going?"

"Bus station. Superstore, Bath. Otherwise Mum will hear tomorrow from that old fellow there about our big shopping tour today."

He's so smart, Ruby thinks to herself. And deep down in her heart she knows already that Cooper has a plan for Cornwall. And that it will work.

4 dead spot – Funkloch

Chapter 10

On their way to the Tate the next morning the sun has vanished as if it had never existed.

Linda is still exhausted from her fight with Jamie over her breakfast cereal. And the weather is not improving her mood[1] either.

Portmeor Beach is deserted, only a few surfers are to be seen at the far end. A light drizzle[2] is in the air.

Linda puts her hood up and sighs. Exactly the weather she expected at a seaside resort. That's what holidays in the United Kingdom always are like: drizzle, the odd[3] shower, rain in places, occasional[4] showers, heavy rain and more rain. She is always surprised about how many different expressions the announcers[5] on the radio provide[6] for the same bad weather conditions: That it's raining again!

Debby has put a nice rain hat on her nice blond hair and is leading as if she knows where to go.

Jamie's attention is caught by a fishing boat lying on the beach. It must be the net with its pattern of rope and knots. He smiles and seems to like the idea of staying here. Only Debby rushes forward to the Gallery and can't stop raving about[7] Josh, the art teacher there.

Linda had bought herself a timeout in her room last night with the promise to take Jamie to the Tate, stay there and see if he likes the course and be responsible for him.

1 mood – Stimmung 2 drizzle – Sprühregen 3 odd – gelegentlich, seltsam 4 occasional – gelegentlich 5 announcer – Sprecher 6 to provide – bereithalten 7 to rave about – schwärmen über/von

Exercise 33

Parallelwelten: Finde die Gegenteilpaare und verbinde sie mit Strichen.

forward	*wrong*
right	*strong*
correct	*backward*
hard	*left*
weak	*soft*

Cooper had been a bit strange on the phone. He insisted on coming to Cornwall although Linda does not have a clue[8] where to hide him and how to fit him into her daily schedule with Jamie and her parents. She will have to call him again, when Jamie is busy at the Tate.

This morning it is easy to get Jamie's attention back to the plan to visit the gallery. Maybe he is exhausted too. He follows them the moment Linda asks him to.

Jamie seems to like Debby and her father, who appeared this morning right in time to interrupt Jamie's fury about Linda. She did not want him to count the cereal loops she was eating from a bowl. Her father was almost freaking out about his kids fighting again and her Mum had been close to tears, when Debby's father knocked.

8 to have a clue – eine Idee haben

Exercise 34

Zeitreise: Setze die Verben in die einfache Vergangenheit (*past tense*, z. B. *went*).

1. *Debby (wears) __________________ a nice rain hat.*
2. *Jamie (eats) __________________ cereal.*
3. *Debby's father (goes) __________________ to the Tate, too.*

He instantly had Jamie's full attention, talked to him about his hobby of building skeletons, as if this was just a normal thing for boys of Jamie's age.

Jamie had showed and explained his work tray and the watchmaker's tools[9] he needs to get the small parts together and they agreed to work together one night on a new project.

Her parents had watched Jamie and Bannister, they had given up their anger about their obnoxious[10] kids and smiled after a while. So Linda had swallowed her bad feelings about Paul Bannister.

"Just Paul," he had told everybody, which Linda found absolutely over the top for 9 o'clock in the morning. That man behaved as if he was at a party! He was just too familiar with everybody, especially Jamie.

Now Debby is speeding up[11] as if the Tate could close any minute.

When they are crossing the street from the beach to the gallery Linda suddenly notices that Jamie is missing. Just a minute ago he was right behind her. Now her brother is gone.

9 watchmaker's tools – Uhrmacherwerkzeug 10 obnoxious – unausstehlich 11 to speed up – beschleunigen

She looks up. The sky has turned even darker after the drizzle and it looks as if a thunderstorm could break out any moment.

Where can Jamie be?

Exercise 35

Viele: Bilde den Plural der folgenden Substantive!

goose ____________________

mouse ____________________

louse ____________________

A lorry blocks her sight of the other side of the street. Most likely something has caught her brother's attention again. It is hard for him to focus on anything which does not come from his own strange perception[12] of things – like the art course. Maybe another fisherman's net or even better: The bare bone[13] of a gigantic shark!

Linda's heartbeat starts stumbling as she rushes across the street and leans over the balustrade. But there is no Jamie.

She turns round. Debby has disappeared inside the Tate. A camper-van stands right behind the lorry. The windscreen wipers are moving, and the driver's door is wide open.

Linda winces[14] at the sight of her brother's pale face behind the windscreen. His eyes and his mouth are wide open. His lips are moving. He must be counting the wipes again. A new fancy[15] of his, she has watched him do this four or five times over the last weeks.

12 perception – Wahrnehmung 13 bone – Knochen, *auch:* Gräte 14 to wince – zusammenzucken
15 fancy – Laune

Exercise 36

Besserwisser: Was ist in den folgenden Sätzen richtig, Adjektiv (z. B. *light, good*) oder Adverb (z. B. *lightly, well*)? Setz die richtige Form ein.

1. *Debby talked (hasty) ________________ about Josh.*
2. *Jamie's smile was (bright) ________________*
3. *Linda's heart beats (irregular) ________________*

Linda rushes across the street and knocks on the camper-van door.

"Here you are! How did you get in?"

"Fifty-three, fifty-four, fifty-five …"

"Is he your brother?" A woman with dark hair and a colourful outfit, perhaps an African caftan, comes forward from the back of the van.

As Linda nods the woman smiles and shakes her head at the same time. "He just stepped in through the open door. My husband has jumped out to get us a flyer from the Gallery. Your brother sat down without a word, watched the wipers and didn't want to talk to me. He seems to be counting the moves. I thought it was best to wait for somebody to come."

"Well, thank you, here I am. Come on Jamie, we have a skeleton to build."

Jamie follows her at once.

Exercise 37

Satzsalat: Bringe die Wörter in die richtige Reihenfolge!

1. *like to Debby her father seems Jamie and.*

   ____

2. *Jamie can Where be?*

   ____

3. *wipes again must be He the counting.*

   ____

The woman gives them both a curious look and moves her hand in front of her face in circles. "Is he mental[16]?"

Linda is used to this gesture.

"No, he is fine. He's just different."

16 mental – geistig, psychisch, *ugs.:* verrückt

Chapter 11

As they enter the Tate they bump into Debby, who has finally realised they were both missing.

With a somehow proud undertone she whispers: "This is it." As if she had built the Gallery.

Linda has to admit that the entrance is impressive. A round glass reception with surrounding stone benches and glass walls that reach up to the third floor. As she looks up she can see the image of Portmeor Beach and the sea reflecting in the glass.

Exercise 38

Zeitreise: Setze die Verben ins Perfekt (*present perfect*, z. B. *has gone*).

1. *The sky (turn) ________________ dark.*
2. *The kids (quarrel) ________________ all day.*
3. *The parents (talk) ________________ behind their backs.*

Jamie seems more attracted by the red floor tiles.

A man of about twenty-five embraces[1] Debby and comes forward to Linda and Jamie.

"So you two want to join our course? Great, great. My name is Josh Burns and I'll show you how to paint and do a bit of sculpting[2]."

1 to embrace – jdn. umarmen, herzen 2 sculpting – Bildhauerei

The guy is tall and slim, with short dark hair. His eyes are dark and soft as chocolate cake. His skin is shimmering like bronze on a statue, and as he smiles at Jamie, Linda thinks he looks a bit like Keanu Reeves in the movie "The Matrix". He is quite handsome[3]. And he appears to know it!

Exercise 39

Besserwisser: Steigere die folgenden Adjektive.

1. *different,* ______________________, ______________________
2. *proud,* ______________________, ______________________
3. *handsome,* ______________________, ______________________

Debby starts speaking about "her work" in an unnatural and high pitched[4] voice. Linda is embarrassed[5]. Josh is far too old for Debby! Can't she see that?

They follow him through several exhibition rooms[6] with large colourful paintings. One of them shows two women with pink and red bathing caps[7].

Another painting is a woman with sunglasses and a hat like a wheel. There are paintings of waves as big as a house, and some naked people. Men and women. All the pictures are quite realistic, which surprises Linda. Small signs beside the paintings explain them and name the painters.

Jamie stops and starts reading. Linda prepares to drag him away and find an excuse for her brother's behaviour. But

3 handsome – attraktiv, gut aussehend 4 high pitched – hoch, schrill 5 to be embarrassed – peinlich berührt sein 6 exhibition room – Ausstellungsraum 7 bathing cap – Badekappe

as Jamie hears Josh talking about sculpting he follows him instantly.

Exercise 40

Wortverdreher: Bilde Fragen aus den folgenden Sätzen, indem du die Wortstellung veränderst und Wörter ergänzt, wo nötig.

1. *Linda is used to this gesture.*

   ____

2. *Josh looks quite handsome.*

   ____

3. *Debby seems to be proud of the teacher.*

   ____

At the end of the exhibition rooms a wooden door leads them into a separate room with four big desks arranged in a square, so that everybody working there can face the others. Three girls about Linda and Debby's age are painting already, one younger boy is working on a separate desk on a limestone[8] statue, which is in a funny stage where it could become almost anything, from a sausage, to a dog or a rocket.

Josh explains what they can do: Paint a picture from a model, as Debby is, paint from fantasy or from an idea he wants to give them.

8 limestone – Kalkstein

Debby walks straight to an easel[9] with a framed canvas and starts preparing a palette with acrylic paint[10] from plastic bottles. Her painting is a still life[11] consisting of three old fashioned cups with saucers[12], of the finest porcelain[13], showing a hunting scene in blue, with an antique silver teapot on feet and a lying bunch of wilting[14] summer flowers in the background. The arrangement is right in front of Debby on a separate table. Her framed canvas[15] shows the sketch of the still life in fine pencil lines, but there is no paint on it. Not yet. Debby sighs like an actress on stage and looks at Josh wistfully[16].

Exercise 41

Zeitreise: Setze die Verben in die Zukunftsform (*future*, z. B. *will go*)!

1. *Jamie and Linda (follow) ________________ Josh through the Tate.*
2. *Debby (is talking) ________________ about how fantastic Josh is.*
3. *Josh (showed) ________________ them how to paint.*

Linda does not want to paint or sculpt at all. She is quite relieved when Josh shrugs his shoulders and excuses himself. He follows Debby's sigh and steps behind her.

Meanwhile Jamie is watching the boy working on the limestone sausage.

9 easel – Staffelei 10 acrylic paint – Acrylfarbe 11 still life – Stillleben 12 saucer – Untertasse 13 porcelain – Porzellan 14 to wilt – verwelken 15 canvas – Leinwand 16 wistfully – sehnsüchtig

"Alex, Alfred, Barbara, Ben, Christopher, Hepworth, Katz, Nicholson, Wallis, Winifred, Wood, 1923, 1925, 1926, 1927, 1933, 1933, 1934 …

Josh turns to Linda. "What is he doing?"

He should know, he is the teacher, Linda thinks, but she clears her throat to reply[17].

Exercise 42

Buchstabensalat: Sortiere die Buchstaben so, dass sinnvolle Wörter entstehen!

1. *hibitexnio* ________________________
2. *aininptg* ________________________
3. *lionestme* ________________________

"Jamie likes to put everything in a special order. Now he is putting the painters in the correct alphabetical order. And the years of their works."

The young sculptor looks at Jamie somehow confused. But as Jamie seems not to want to talk to him, he turns back and goes on filing at the stone.

"Are you okay?" She asks her brother.

Jamie nods. "I like this gallery."

"Do you want to stay?"

"Yes. Maybe we can work on a skeleton. You said so."

"Maybe." Linda has her doubts.

17 to reply – antworten

A minute later Josh has returned to Jamie and puts his arm around his shoulders.

"You remember all the names and dates on the signs? That's absolutely stunning[18]! You're brilliant! And you want to work on a skeleton? Tell me everything about your concept."

Josh Burns seems to like Jamie. Not like the woman in the camper-van. Linda can leave her brother with this guy, nothing bad will happen. Linda is not totally convinced of this, but she has to talk to Cooper soon.

As she indicates[19] by putting an imaginative mobile phone to her ear, Josh answers with a smile and a wave of his hands.

Exercise 43

Nicht dürfen: Übersetze die folgenden Sätze.

1. *Du darfst Jamie nicht alleine lassen.*

   ____

2. *Er darf nicht mit toten Tieren spielen.*

   ____

3. *Debby darf nicht mit Josh flirten.*

   ____

18 stunning – atemberaubend, verblüffend 19 to indicate – zu verstehen geben

Chapter 12

That guy is friendly.

Hmmm, hmmm …

You know the expression on his face from the little book.
You don't have to look it up right now.
You know the signs.
His eyes are wide open.

Hmm, hmmm …

He looks at you.
Bolt?

Exercise 44

Lückenfüller: Setze die richtigen Präpositionen ein!

1. *Debby sighs like Juliet __________ stage and looks __________ Josh wistfully.*
2. *They can paint __________ a model, __________ fantasy or __________ an idea.*
3. *The young sculptor looks __________ Jamie somehow confused.*

But not too long.

The corners of his mouth[1] are lifted upwards.

That is a smile.

Hmm, hmmm.

He has touched your shoulders.

Bolt?

But only a second.

You can see his hands.

He is wearing a blue shirt and blue jeans.

He is interested in skeletons.

He is a good guy.

He can be relied on[2].

Exercise 45

Besserwisser: Welche der folgenden Aussagen ist falsch?

1. *Jamie goes into a camper-van without being invited.*
2. *Debby's brother is at the Tate, too.*
3. *Linda wants to leave Jamie at the course.*

Hmmm, hmmm...

1 corner of the mouth – Mundwinkel 2 to rely on s.o. – jmd. vertrauen

Chapter 13

"You are nuts[1]! You can't come here!"

Linda has to quiet down her voice. Everybody in the café on the roof of the Tate Gallery is watching her screaming into her mobile phone.

Exercise 46

Hauptsache: Unterstreiche die Substantive (keine Namen!) im vorigen Absatz und setze sie in den Plural bzw. Singular.

____

____

____

"You have to get back home, wait …"

Cooper interrupts her. Linda can hardly understand him. He must be standing on the train, there is a rattling noise next to him as if a door was closing.

"I can't. Our parents are coming home this afternoon, and if I don't leave now they will …"

As Cooper pauses she watches the waitress stumble over a guest's foot. She drops her tray and spills a big cup of white coffee and some scones[2] over a lady in a yellow summer dress.

1 to be nuts – verrückt sein, spinnen 2 scone – süßes brötchenartiges Gebäck

The lady screams and jumps up from her chair, hitting the table which causes even more trouble: A glass of water falls over[3] and wets the trousers of her husband.

"What a mess," Linda whispers.

Exercise 47

Lückenfüller: Ergänze das fehlende Wort!

1. *Debby's painting is a ______________*
2. *The young sculptor is working on a ______________ sausage.*
3. *The ______________ stumbles and spills coffee over a lady.*

"Yeah, too true," Cooper replies. "I have my sleeping bag with me and there is a Backpacker's[4] in St Ives, where I can stay. Don't worry. I'll arrive at Penzance at about 8 o'clock. Might be in St Ives around 9 or 10 tonight. Don't switch your mobile off, just switch off the sound[5]."

Then Cooper is gone.

Linda cannot believe that he is already on his way. Something must have happened. Usually Cooper listens to what she says. Why is he so stubborn this time? What was he going to say? His parents will what? Keep him from following her?

Oh, Cooper! I really want to see you, but we have to be careful! If my parents catch us[6] together they will send you home, instantly! And they will take my mobile from me, Linda thinks.

She has to call Ruby again.

3 to fall over – umkippen 4 Backpacker's – Unterkunft für Rucksackreisende 5 to switch off the sound – den Ton abschalten 6 to catch s.o. – jmd. erwischen

Exercise 48

Verbbeuger: Ergänze die fehlenden Konjunktionsformen der folgenden Verben (z. B. *go, went, gone*).

1. ____________________, *took*, ____________________
2. *catch*, ____________________, ____________________
3. ____________________, ____________________, *stood*

Linda watches the waitress trying to help the lady clean her yellow dress. But the coffee stains cannot be removed by wiping[7] them with a paper towel. And the lady's husband does not look any better. As he stands there with the wet spot right in the middle of his trousers his wife starts laughing. At first he looks angry, but after a moment he joins in.

Exercise 49

Strippenzieher: Verbinde die folgenden *phrasal verbs* (Verb mit Partikel) mit der richtigen deutschen Übersetzung.

call for sth.	*nach etw. verlangen*
call off	*ausführen*
carry on	*absagen*
carry out	*weitermachen*

7 to wipe – wischen

The waitress looks from one to the other, not knowing what to think of the matter. Finally she tries a smile, stammers some excuses and offers to pay for the cleaning.

"It's okay," the woman says and puts a note on the table. "It's okay."

I wished I could say that, too, Linda thinks.

Ruby was different on the phone last night. She had sounded as if something else was wrong, apart from their parents coming back from their holiday a day early.

What could that be? As Linda tries to figure out[8] what was wrong last night her first idea is that Ruby was angry.

Was she angry about Linda? But why?

Because Linda had left them with all the tidying up[9] after the party?

Exercise 50

Lückenfüller: Häng das passende Frageanhängsel (*question tag*, z. B. *You haven't seen her, have you?*) an.

1. *The waitress is trying to give the lady a hand,* _______________?
2. *Linda wonders why Ruby was so strange,* _______________?
3. *Ruby was not friendly,* _______________?

But Ruby knew that Linda had to be home early. The same rules apply[10] to all her friends of her own age. Although Ruby has a big brother, who is allowed to do almost everything, so she should be

8 to figure out – rauskriegen 9 to tidy up – aufräumen 10 to apply to – gelten für

in a better position to argue with her parents than friends without elder brothers. But she always has to be at home before midnight.

And Ruby also knew that Linda's family was leaving early the next morning for their summer holiday in damned Cornwall. So what could she be angry about now?

Linda has no choice. She has to call Ruby. To ask her what is wrong and why Cooper cannot wait until Linda figures out how they can meet without being discovered.

Ruby, her best friend. She always knows what to do.

Chapter 14

"No, I'm not angry. At least not angry with you," Ruby says.

Linda can imagine how she is frowning. Her voice is not back to normal, although she tries to hide whatever is gnawing at[1] her.

Linda does not want to appear whiny[2], but she has to find out what's happened in Bath that made Cooper forget what they had agreed upon before Linda left: to wait until she gave the okay for his arrival in Cornwall.

"So why did you hang up last night?"

"It was just because ..., well ..., you see. Cooper wanted me to lie for him to our parents. Tell them he is in Scotland with Franklin and his family. He has never done such a thing before, no matter how stupid the action he was trying to hide. He always did it on his own, without roping me in[3]. And even when he said he would write a letter for our parents, which – by the way – he didn't do, I had the impression that he had done something really ..."

"Really what, Ruby?"

"Really stupid. I don't know," Ruby says. "And I have a very strong feeling that he did not forget to write that letter but that he did it on purpose[4]."

"So what do you think has happened? I mean, there was the party, all right. I was there. You were there, too. What could he have done, that you don't know about?"

Linda can hear Ruby pushing something around on an even surface, maybe the vase of flowers her mother always arranges on the kitchen table.

1 to gnaw at – an etwas nagen 2 whiny - weinerlich 3 to rope in – hineinziehen 4 to do s.th. on purpose – etwas absichtlich tun

Exercise 51

Just do it: Unterstreiche die Verben im vorigen Absatz und konjugiere sie durch.

____

____

"I have no idea. He helped tidy up, went shopping, prepared everything for our parents. And left this morning in a hurry. To meet you. You are the one who should know what he is up to, you are closer to him than me, his sister."

Linda feels as if they are going around in circles, pushing responsibility from one to the other: You should know, you are closer to him … like the sea vortex[5] in one of the paintings they saw on their way to the painting course.

"Oh, come on, Ruby! He is on the train already! I didn't know anything about it! My mother will freak out, if she sees him here! What shall I do? Haven't you got an idea?"

"Time will tell. Wait and see. Cooper can look after himself. You don't have to care for him. He has travelled on his own before. He will find a way to get to you, you can bet[6] on that."

"I'm sure he will. But I'm not sure if I like the idea. My parents will think I planned it."

"What you haven't, together with Cooper? Are you trying to sell this story to me?"

"Oh, come on Ruby. You know quite well that I'm just trying not to hurt anybody, to take care of my little brother, to give my

5 vortex – Strudel, Wirbel 6 to bet on s.th. – auf etwas wetten

parents a rest so that they can settle their problems. Is it so bad that I want to see my boyfriend Cooper as well? To have some fun under all this pressure?"

Exercise 52

Was wäre, wenn: Ergänze die fehlenden Verbformen in den folgenden If-Sätzen (Typ 1).

1. *If Cooper (tell) ________________ the truth, Ruby will not have to lie.*
2. *If Ruby (tell) ________________ her everything, Linda will not have to ask her about Cooper.*
3. *If Cooper stays at home, nobody (have) ________________ to worry.*

Chapter 15

"Look at those seals[1] over there!" Their mother points over the cliffs. Down in the foaming[2] waves two black spots are to be seen. Linda cannot figure out whether they are animals or just some buoys[3].

"Uhum ..."

"The sun is hanging over the lighthouse! Look, how lovely!"

Linda is not interested in seals or lovely views at all. She has to watch her step. She does not have a single moment left for the outstanding natural beauty her parents are so crazy about[4]. The coastal path leading from the graveyard in St Ives to a place called Zennor is rocky and muddy.

"Puddles in places," she murmurs thinking of the announcer's creativity with names for rain on the radio.

"If we are lucky, we'll see some dolphins," her father takes over in a useless attempt to cheer the kids up.

Jamie has already stumbled over a rock. His knee is bleeding and he is counting, maybe his steps. He is not in the best mood and has already shouted "bolt, bolt, bolt!" at Linda when she tried to clean the wound.

When they crossed Portmeor Beach on their way to the beginning of the coastal path half an hour ago he had stopped by the fishing boat they had seen that morning. It had disappeared when they went home after the arts course, but had returned to the same place in the afternoon.

This time the fisherman was there, working on a net. A big

1 seal – Seehund 2 to foam – schäumen 3 buoy – Boje 4 to be crazy about – verrückt sein nach

dead fish, as long as Jamie's arm, was lying beside the boat. Jamie wanted to talk about the fish, perhaps to find out about the possibility of getting its bones.

Exercise 53

„Am Lesen sein": Setze die folgenden Verben in die Verlaufsform.

1. *The sun (rises)* ____________________
2. *The surfers (surf)* ____________________
3. *The kids (complain)* ____________________

The fisherman turned out to be the lighthouse keeper[5], not of Godrevy lighthouse which their mother had just pointed at in the far distance, but of the smaller lighthouse on the St Ives' harbour pier.

He is a sturdy[6] man, not much taller than Linda, with a face like an old leather handbag and a nose like a potato under a bunch of hair like faded out[7] yellow cotton wool. His left eye is somehow crippled[8], a scar[9] running over it, from his forehead to the side of his nose, so that he cannot close the lid[10]. But the eyeball is not hurt. It seems to bulge out[11] of his face, a big white ball with a little very bright blue in the middle. Although the other eye is normal, the man looks a bit mad[12], and now as Linda remembers him, she is ashamed how prejudiced she was just by his looks. He had perhaps had a fishing accident and is unhappy about his scar, but absolutely healthy inside his head.

5 lighthouse keeper – Leuchtturmwärter 6 sturdy – stämmig 7 faded out – ausgebleicht 8 crippled – verkrüppelt 9 scar – Narbe 10 lid, eyelid – Augenlid 11 to bulge out – sich vorwölben 12 mad – verrückt

Exercise 54

Zukunftsmusik: Bilde die Zukunftsform, die eine feste Absicht ausdrückt oder unmittelbar bevorsteht (mit *going to*).

1. *The seals (dive) ________________ away.*
2. *The fisherman (leave) ________________ the beach.*
3. *The family (walk) ________________ the coastal path.*

Their father exchanged a few words with the man, asked if he liked the work at the lighthouse, if it wasn't too boring. The keeper – his name is Angus – had not been very talkative. But he had smiled at Jamie and taken the boy's hand. He had moved it over the dead fish as if stroking a pet. Jamie had liked this, but their father had seemed embarrassed[13] and dragged Jamie forward.

This walk appears to be her parents' family event of the day. "I need a bit of a family feeling today, that's what holidays are for, aren't they?" her father had said and her mother had agreed: "You are so right, Matthew. And you kids could try and cooperate without complaining."

Okay, okay. They are trying hard not to complain. Even Jamie is trying meanwhile.

Linda holds her mobile phone in her hand, just in case it starts vibrating, when Cooper calls, but it is too early. He will still be on the train to Penzance. She is stumbling forward.

The sky is dark again, but it is not too cold. Which is good, as it will soon start raining again.

13 to be embarrassed – peinlich berührt sein

Exercise 55

Was wäre, wenn: Ergänze die fehlenden Verbformen in den folgenden If-Sätzen (Typ 2).

1. *If the fisherman went away, the family (walk) ______________ the coastal path.*
2. *If Josh built a skeleton, Jamie (admire) ______________ him.*
3. *If Cooper was there, Linda (argue) ______________ with him.*

"How far is this village anyhow? And why are we going there?" she asks.

Her father sighs. "We'll need one more hour. The village is where a famous author used to live, D. H. Laurence, with his German wife. We are going there because of the Mermaid's Chair in the church. You will like it, Linda."

"There is a very romatic story about this chair, with a – was it a priest, Matthew?" her mother goes on.

"No, it was a chorister, I think, and the mermaid … well, let's wait until we see the chair. You will be impressed!"

You bet, Linda thinks, I'm absolutely crazy about all kinds of fairy tales[14]! But she doesn't say it aloud.

They walk in silence the rest of the way. Her mother grabs her father's hand and they talk in low voices. Linda wonders what they are talking about.

14 fairy tale – Märchen

Exercise 56

Können und dürfen: Übersetze die folgenden Sätze und verwende *to be able to* oder *to be allowed to*.

1. *Können sich die Kinder beklagen?*

   ____

2. *Kann Jamie alleine in die Tate gehen?*

   ____

3. *Kann Linda ihren kleinen Bruder tragen?*

   ____

Chapter 16

The Mermaid's Chair is an old seat made out of dark wood, standing in a side aisle[1] of the ancient St Senara's Church. Linda's father is in his best mood. And he is well prepared. She can judge this from the determined expression on his face. Determined to tell them the story.

"Look at these carvings[2]," he exclaims.

Even Jamie bows forward, but Linda is convinced he is not examining the carving but counting the pattern. While he is doing this he taps[3] her elbow with one finger. He has been doing this since they arrived in this village by the sea, a quick and strong rhythm that is getting on her nerves.

"Oh Matthew," their mother whispers and points to the tapestry[4] cushion on the seat. "Have you seen the lovely cushion?"

Of course, they all have seen the cushion, they are not blind! There are hundreds of these cushions lying in the bench rows, all looking colourful and individual, as if every family has its own. But the cushion on the Mermaid Chair is special. Five fish, indicating that this has got something to do with the sea. What a surprise!

"Well, my name, Matthew, is the keyword to the story." Their father waves at them to take a seat.

Jamie takes one of the cushions on his lap and starts feeling over the small elevations, perhaps counting the knots in the tapestry pattern.

1 aisle – Seitenschiff 2 carving – Schnitzerei; to carve – schnitzen 3 to tap – klopfen 4 tapestry – Gobelin

Linda closes her fingers even more strongly around the mobile phone in her jeans to calm herself down and look as if she is concentrating on her Dad's lecture.

Exercise 57

Müssen: Übersetze die folgenden Sätze und setze die korrekte Form von *must* oder *have to* ein.

1. *Musst du so laut sein?*

   ____

2. *Du musst vor 10 Uhr hier sein!*

   ____

3. *Du darfst deine Eltern nicht belügen!*

   ____

"This church, or at least the basis of it, dates back to the 6th century, and so does the Mermaid Chair. The carving shows a mermaid with an apple in one hand and a comb in the other. You have to know the history of this symbol."

Do I really have to know that? Linda opens her eyes wide to keep herself from falling asleep.

Her father continues.

"Before the Christian age, mermaids were connected with Aphrodite, the goddess of the sea and of love. But when the Christians came, they changed the apple into a mirror and said mermaids were a symbol of vanity[5] and heartlessness.

Exercise 58

Nicht müssen: Bilde die Verneinung der folgenden Sätze.

1. *Du musst das nicht aufessen.*

   ____

2. *Du musst das Buch nicht lesen.*

   ____

3. *Wir müssen nicht nach Zennor gehen.*

   ____

After that a double meaning was left to the figure: As she was half human and half fish people believed she was close to Jesus Christ, who was half God, half human.

However, the Zennor mermaid was attracted by the singing of a chorister[6]."

Their father makes a dramatic pause and looks at their faces to see if everybody is listening. Only Jamie does not look back, but that is acceptable. Linda gives her face a deeply interested expression and her mother gasps[7] with tension[8].

"This is where my name comes into play[9]. This chorister's name was ..." He stops and points his index finger at Linda.

"Matthew," she hisses[10].

5 vanity – Eitelkeit 6 chorister – Chorsänger 7 to gasp – hörbar einatmen 8 tension – Anspannung 9 to come into play – ins Spiel kommen 10 to hiss – fauchen, zischen

"Exactly. Matthew Trewhella was his name. And the mermaid left the sea and came to listen to his beautiful voice every Sunday night. Weeks went by. But one night she couldn't stand her longing for his voice any longer. So she lured[11] him out of the church and along the river to the sea. And Matthew followed her. He was never seen again."

Exercise 59

Nicht dürfen: Übersetze die folgenden Sätze.

1. *Sie dürfen nicht bei Nacht an den Strand (gehen).*

   ____

2. *Wir dürfen die Türen nicht offen lassen.*

   ____

3. *Ich darf nicht zu spät kommen.*

   ____

Her mother sighs. "What a moving story."

"Yes, and on warm summer nights, like today, you can hear the two lovers' voices singing down by the Mermaid's Cove. Imagine the sweetness. And that's where we are going right now."

Linda tries to imagine Cooper singing a love song. That's not sweet, not sweet at all. But cool. And exciting. Linda grabs the front of her T-shirt and concentrates. As she almost hears his

11 to lure – locken

voice, a sound of something huge falling or bursting shakes the ground. A vibration runs up her legs. She feels for her mother's hand. But there is nothing.

Her parents jump up from their seats. At the back of the church some people start screaming.

Linda looks around to figure out what has happened.

"Jamie! Where is Jamie?" her mother yells[12].

Linda cannot see him.

There is a lot of dust lingering in the air.

"Jamie!"

Exercise 60

Fundstücke: Finde im Anfang des Kapitels die englischen Entsprechungen zu diesen Sätzen.

1. *Ja, klar haben sie alle das Kissen gesehen, sie sind ja nicht blind!*
2. *Ihr müsst die Geschichte dieses Symbols kennen.*
3. *Doch eines Nachts konnte sie ihre Sehnsucht nach seiner Stimme nicht länger ertragen.*

12 to yell – gellend schreien

Chapter 17

"Where, for God's sake, is my car?" Ruby's father comes running into the house. "The garage is empty! What have you done to my brand new car? And where is Cooper, where is your brother?"

Ruby cowers[1] in one corner of the sofa, wraps her arms around her knees and hopes her father will calm down soon. Her mother has dropped by her side.

Everything seemed okay when her parents arrived from the airport. They were suntanned, everything had gone fine with the flight and the taxi, they had accepted that Cooper had left with a friend. Ruby had been as vague as possible, but now she would have to tell the whole lie. But she didn't want to. Why hadn't Cooper written the letter, as he had promised?

Her parents had looked in the fridge and in every room and both seemed to be satisfied with the condition of the house. Ruby had been so happy.

Until her father wanted to take the car to drive to the office for a short look at what had happened over the last two weeks.

"I have no idea about your car," Ruby says when her father has to pause to take a deep breath." We didn't even use our bikes over the last few days. I haven't been in the garage for ages. What is wrong?"

"It is gone!" her father cried. "There is no cursed[2] car in our garage! Absolutely! No car! Do you hear me? Did Cooper take it?"

Oh my goodness, Ruby thinks. Has he?

1 to cower – zusammenkauern 2 cursed – verdammt

"N.. nno, he …, well, he took the train, as far as I know," is all she can say.

Exercise 61

Wessen? Setze die folgenden Begriffe in den Genitiv.

1. *the Mermaid + Chair*

   ____

2. *the students + courses*

   ____

3. *the horse + saddle*

   ____

Her mother puts her hand on Ruby's knee and squeezes it consolingly[3].

Ruby knows that Cooper sometimes took the old car, although he doesn't have a driving licence. But she has never seen him take the new SUV.

Her father runs around in the living room, he opens the terrace door and steps outside. As if he could find his beloved car in the garden.

"He has taken the train to follow Franklin, you say? To Scotland? Oh sugar[4]! You know, the whole highlands are a dead spot! When did he leave?"

3 consoling – tröstend 4 sugar – *ugs. Ersatz für:* „shit"

Ruby doesn't want to lie, but she has to say something. So she stays as close to the truth as possible.

"Early this morning. He should still be on the train."

Her father is already pressing the buttons of the phone. "If I don't reach him, I'll call Franklin's parents!"

Exercise 62

Zeitreise: Setze die folgenden Verben ins Präsens.

1. *The mermaid (came) ________________ to lure the man into the sea.*
2. *The family (listened) ________________ carefully.*
3. *Jamie (had vanished) ________________ out of sight.*

God, why doesn't Cooper call, and help her out of this dilemma? He must know how his father is.

Ruby watches her father walking up and down in the living room, while waiting for Cooper to answer the phone.

"Busy[5]."

He presses the red button and throws angry looks at Ruby.

A second later the phone in his hand rings. Her father looks at the display.

"That's him," he says and barks[6] "yes" into the receiver.

5 busy – besetzt 6 to bark – bellen

Chapter 18

Slowly the dust settles. A group of people has gathered around the place where the Mermaid Chair stands.

Ruby steps beside her mother and looks at her father, who is bowing down to the ground. Jamie's feet are moving, but the rest of his body is covered by a tapestry. Jamie is screaming, "bolt, bolt, bolt …".

People help to take the carpet from her brother. The Mermaid Chair has dropped to the side. An old man in a black frock[1] is lamenting[2], "Oh dear Jesus, how could this happen?" He waves both hands above his head.

Their Dad is examining Jamie, who seems to be unhurt[3], then he moves him into Linda's arms.

"You take care of him now!"

Linda takes Jamie's hand and drags him towards the entrance, while her parents talk to the man in black, who is obviously the parish priest[4].

Jamie is still agitated[5], he cannot stop saying, "Bolt, bolt, bolt…", but he follows Linda.

The way home is not better than the way they came. The Mermaid Chair is unbroken. Obviously Jamie had tried to look where the carvings ended under the wooden sides of the seat and his hands had not been strong enough to keep it in balance when he pushed it upwards. Unfortunately the tapestry was hit by the falling seat.

1 frock – Kutte 2 to lament – jammern 3 unhurt – unverletzt 4 parish priest – Pfarrer 5 agitated – sehr erregt

Exercise 63

Parallelwelten: Finde die Gegenteilpaare und verbinde sie mit Strichen.

open	*under*
left	*dressed*
above	*behind*
in front	*right*
naked	*close*

The priest and their parents had managed to put the seat and the wall carpet up again. But everybody looks grey from the dust and as they walk to the Zennor bus stop their father doesn't talk any more.

The bus stops right in front of the Backpacker's in St Ives. Linda is the last to get off the bus. She turns her back to their parents and types a short text message to Cooper:

"Found the Backpacker's. Just text me when you are there."

Her mother freaks out as she realises that Linda is texting. "On the internet again? Facebook again? Defaming[6] your poor brother again? He is just different! When will you get that?"

Linda swallows heavily. She has never ever defamed her brother. She cancelled her Facebook account weeks ago because she couldn't save photos there. But her mother will never understand.

"I just texted Ruby about our walk today. That's all. Sorry!"

6 to defame – diffamieren

Exercise 64

Zeitreise: Setze die Verben in die einfache Vergangenheit (*past tense*, z. B. *went*).

1. *Linda (takes) ________________ Jamie's hand and (drags) ________________ him towards the entrance.*
2. *Jamie (leaves) ________________ the church.*
3. *Their father (shakes) ________________ his head.*

Her father just shakes his head. He looks depressed.

They all go into the supermarket, to buy some spuds[7], some vegetables and a chicken. This is Jamie's wish. He needs the bones, for the art class next morning.

After her father has paid he pulls himself together[8] and says: "That's not too bad: A grilled chicken, my favourite, that's a perspective for a nice meal at least."

Exercise 65

Viele: Bilde den Plural der folgenden Substantive.

bus ________________

policeman ________________

gallery ________________

7 spud – *ugs. für:* Kartoffeln 8 to pull o.s. together – sich zusammenreißen

But a second later he learns from his wife that it will be chicken soup, since Jamie needs the bones boiled, not grilled, because they get cleaner that way.

From that moment onwards both their parents don't talk any more. Not during the preparations for dinner, not during the meal, not even when Jamie assembles[9] all the bones on the table while they are still eating.

"Look, how clean they are," Jamie lifts the bare chicken bones and fondles[10] the ends of the chicken legs.

He is right, Linda has to admit to herself. These parts get brown and ugly on a grilled chicken. At the same moment she calls herself insane.

Right after dinner Linda and Jamie are sent to their rooms. Which is welcomed by Linda as she can text Cooper, who is in Penzance now and looking for a transfer possibility to St Ives.

Through the half closed door of her room Linda can hear her parents talk.

EXERCISE 66

Besserwisser: Was ist in den folgenden Sätzen richtig, Adjektiv (z. B. *light, good*) oder Adverb (z. B. *lightly, well*)? Setz die richtige Form ein.

1. *The Mermaid Chair is (wonderful) ________________ carved.*
2. *The fisherman has a (horrible) ________________ scar across his face.*
3. *Linda's father wants his chicken (fresh) ________________ grilled.*

9 to assemble – zusammensetzen 10 to fondle – liebkosen

Her father gets loud every once in a while, Linda hears "I'm fed up, totally fed up, this is no holiday, this is torture!" several times. And he goes on, "He will never learn, as long as you can't let go[11]! The disaster with the Mermaid Chair wouldn't have happened if we hadn't forced him to go into that damned Zennor church with us. And the same is true for Linda! Why should she feel responsible for her brother, when you always hover[12] around them."

Her mother stays calm. Linda can hardly understand what she says. But she feels sorry and angry about her father. And she wishes they would find a way not to fight about Jamie and herself.

An hour later they come to her to tell her they are leaving for a beer at the pub.

Linda agrees at once to stay with Jamie at the apartment.

Exercise 67

Satzsalat: Bringe die Wörter in die richtige Reihenfolge!

1. *all go the into they supermarket.*

____

2. *the art the needs for bones Jamie class.*

____

3. *every in a father gets her while loud once.*

____

11 to let go – loslassen 12 to hover – *fig.:* schweben über

Chapter 19

"So you didn't take the car, Cooper? Then I have to call the police! Cooper? Cooper!" Ruby's father stares at the receiver.

"Blimey[1]! He's gone! First the connection was really poor, then he was just gone!"

Her mother jumps in.

"You know about the dead spots yourself. Remember your last trip to Scotland, dear."

Or Cooper just hung up, Ruby thinks, but she doesn't say it out loud.

"You're right, and I could hear the train in the background. Okay."

Ruby's stomach is aching. She feels sick and has to run to the bathroom.

After a while and a lot of cold water running over her forearms, she feels a bit better. She sits down on the toilet cover. What if her visions were true and Jamie had been in her father's car? If Jamie had managed to take the car and damaged it? And left it somewhere?

No, Jamie is in Cornwall right now, and Linda didn't tell her he was injured[2] or anything – well somehow sick or strange or different from – normal. From his usual condition.

No, Jamie couldn't have taken her father's car. Could he?

And Cooper? Could he? To take Melinda home?

Oh dear me, Ruby thinks, if I only could be sure what I'd seen! But wouldn't Cooper have told me if he had taken Dad's car?

1 blimey – *ugs.* Himmelherrgottnochmal! 2 injured – *verletzt*

And wouldn't he have brought it back? I'll have to ask him.

Right now.

Exercise 68

Zeitreise: Setze die Verben ins Perfekt (*present perfect*, z. B. *has gone*).

1. *Cooper (takes) __________________ the train to Penzance in the end.*
2. *Ruby (is fed up) __________________ with her brother at bedtime.*
3. *Ruby (tries) __________________ to call Cooper three times.*

Ruby goes back to the living room and takes her mobile. Her parents are in the kitchen. She can hear her father speak on the phone. He is spelling the name of the road they live on, perhaps to the police.

In her room Ruby presses Cooper's quick dial[3]. But she only gets the answer: "The person you called is momentarily not available."

And his voicemail[4] is switched off, too.

He is so smart, her brother! By having done that he is absolutely out of his parent's reach. But out of hers as well.

3 quick dial – Kurzwahltaste 4 voicemail – Mobilbox

Chapter 20

No, don't look out of the window, Jamie. No!

Bolt! Bolt!

There are bright rays in the dark sky. They will hurt you. And you can't switch them off like your mobile phone.

Hmmm, hmmm …

Stay focussed on the bird in front of you, just stay focussed.

Start with the names of the bones. Later on you can say them in the opposite order, from Z to A.

Hmmm, hmm …

And after that you can even count them.

Look at those bones! That looks nice. Very nice.

You will need new glue and a new plate to ground it on. And wire[1].

Cervicalvertebrae?

1 wire – Draht

Exercise 69

Besserwisser: Steigere die folgenden Adjektive.

1. *large,* __________________, __________________
2. *big,* __________________, __________________
3. *sunny,* __________________, __________________

Bolt? Bolt?

Cervicalvertebrae …

Hmmm …

Cervicalvertebrae, coracoid[2], digit[3], femur[4], fourth digit[5], furcula[6], hallux[7], humerus[8], pygostyle[9], pubis[10] …

Hmmm…

2–10 *Bezeichnungen für Knochen im Vogelskelett*

Chapter 21

Linda is fast asleep when her parents wake her up early in the morning.

"What's wrong?" she murmurs.

She hadn't slept too well with the knowledge that Cooper is at the Backpacker's only a few streets away. Just talking on the phone the night before seemed to be such a waste of time!

And if it had not been for Jamie's safety at the apartment and for the risk of running into her parents by the harbour, where their favourite pub "The Sloop Inn" was situated, Linda would have gone to meet him.

"What time is it?" she mumbles and hides under her duvet[1].

"Only 7," her mother says, "but you must get up. We have to talk."

Jamie is already sitting at the breakfast table, fully dressed, shuffling the chicken bones around on the table, when Linda sits down, still in her pyjamas, rubbing the sleepiness from her eyes.

Her Mum puts a firmly stuffed backpack on the table.

Oh, no, Linda thinks. Not another family trip! What am I to do about Cooper? I need to see him soon!

She does not dare to ask, but she remembers her parents mentioning an educational park somewhere close by: the "Eden Project", and another fantastic and even larger beach than the one right in front of their kitchen window, Carbis Beach in the next village. Perhaps another walk along the damned coastal path. And there are even more places her Mum would like to

1 duvet – Bettdecke, Plumeau

visit, where another author was born or lived or died, her name was Rosamunde Pilcher or whatever …

Exercise 70

Wortverdreher: Bilde Fragen aus den folgenden Sätzen, indem du die Wortstellung veränderst und Wörter ergänzt, wo nötig.

1. *Linda is fast asleep.*

   ____

2. *She hides under her duvet.*

   ____

3. *There are more places her mother would like to visit.*

   ____

Linda thinks she will never see Cooper again, she will get lost in her parent's stupid argument about how family affairs should be dealt with, how conflicts should be settled, no matter what the children have on their own minds.

Linda is fed up, too, like her father, but their parents are not interested in her feelings. Nobody is. Nobody, apart from Cooper. And Ruby, maybe.

Jamie is playing with the cereal loops on the table. He is making up a new arrangement out of his cereal, combining it with the chicken bones. Linda has to refrain[2] from laughing out

2 to refrain – sich verkneifen

loud. This newest arrangement reminds her of a circus with some skinny artists juggling[3] with car tyres[4].

"So where do we have to go today?" she asks fearfully after watching Jamie for a while.

Exercise 71

Zeitreise: Setze die Verben in die Zukunftsform (*future*, z.B. *will go*).

1. *Linda (gets) ________________ up.*
2. *Jamie (drinks) ________________ a glass of milk.*
3. *Their parents (travel) ________________ around.*

"You're not going anywhere," their father replies. "Only to the Tate Gallery for the art course. And wherever you two would like to go if you could decide for yourselves. Your Mum and I are going to the Isles of Scilly. We told you about that, but you two seem to be happy here. And we don't want to miss this opportunity."

Linda feels her face brightening up and she tries to hide her happiness instantly.

Their mother takes over.

"You know, Daddy is so keen on birds and I'm so interested in rare flowers. Both can be seen on the Scillies. We decided to go there today. The transfer from St Ives to Penzance only goes on Wednesdays, and the weather this week is calm enough to

3 to juggle – jonglieren 4 tyre – Reifen

take the ferry. That is not advisable when the sea is rough, but the weather will be calm for the next few days. So this is the only safe opportunity for us, next week the weather might be too bad."

Their mother looks concerned, but their father goes on.

Exercise 72

Buchstabensalat: Sortiere die Buchstaben so, dass sinnvolle Wörter entstehen!

1. *daedWensy* ______________________
2. *potutyropni* ______________________
3. *teunhassim* ______________________

"You two can manage two days on your own, can't you?"

Jamie nods fiercely and Linda has to swallow down a Yippiee-iyeah! She covers her face briefly with both hands and then looks at her parents with what she thinks is a patient[5] smile.

"No problem. The course at the Tate is half a day, with an invitation to come back after lunch. The fridge is filled, and in the late afternoon we can go to the beach or the harbour. Jamie likes the fishing boats. What do you think, Jamie?"

"Yes, I love the birds and the boats. That's fine."

Their father hesitates a moment and Linda starts to fear they might decide otherwise. So she gets up and pushes Jamie softly into the ribs.

5 patient – geduldig

"Shall we see these two to the bus station? Near the supermarket? What do you think?"

"Yeah, let's go." Jamie looks back to the arrangement on the table, but for some strange reason he is cooperating this morning, as if he wanted their parents to leave as well.

"We will be back tomorrow by 8 pm, so it would be great if you two came for us[6]. Here are fifty pounds, just in case you want an ice cream or anything else. Keep the receipts[7], if you have to buy anything more expensive than …" their father looks at their mother, "let's say 10 pounds, okay?"

Their mother nods and their father goes on, "and if anything happens, you can call us any time. Or just ask Paul Bannister for help. We met him last night at "The Sloop Inn". He knows where we are."

Their mother puts her arms around Jamie, "and you, young man, switch your mobile phone on and leave it on. I know, you don't like that, but it is necessary for your safety, okay?"

Jamie nods slowly, takes the phone from the pocket of his shorts, switches it on, then he puts it on the table.

Linda is sure he will leave it there and only stuff it back into his shorts after he switched it off again.

Half an hour later they stand in the early morning sunshine in front of the Backpacker's and wave their parents goodbye.

6 to come for s.o. – jmd. abholen 7 receipt – Rechnungsbeleg, Quittung

Chapter 22

Linda would prefer to walk into the Backpacker's and surprise Cooper, but there is no chance of leaving Jamie alone outside. There is nothing she could keep him busy with like counting tiles or bricks[1]. All the surfaces of the surrounding houses are even, and there is nothing else to attract his attention. And she can't take him inside. The risk that Jamie might tell their parents the following night about Cooper being in St Ives, is far too big.

So they get some scones and clotted cream[2] for a cream tea breakfast to celebrate their freedom. Jamie is in a brilliant mood and talks about the art course and how nice Josh and Debby are. Which is quite unusual for him, he is not much of a talker. Linda is confused about this change in his behaviour.

Did he understand what their parents talked about last night, too? Is he aware[3] that their parents do not accept both of them as they are? Is he willing and, what is more important, able to change himself? Is her picture of her little brother wrong?

An hour later they walk along Portmeor Beach towards the Tate Gallery. It is high tide. Most of the rocks are hidden now under the surface and the surfers are chasing the perfect wave, which must be among those waves, they are really huge this morning.

It is still a bit cool, but the sun is out. Only a few clouds are gathering on the opposite side of the bay. Hopefully they will dissolve and the weather will stay nice. Linda is determined to take Cooper up the small peninsula[4] at the back of their apartment block. The people here call the peninsula "The Island".

1 brick – Backstein 2 clotted cream – besonders reichhaltige Sahne, ähnlich wie Schmand 3 to be aware – sich bewusst sein 4 peninsula – Halbinsel

Exercise 73

Lückenfüller: Setze die richtigen Präpositionen ein!

1. *Jamie is not much __________ a talker.*
2. *An hour later they walk __________ Portmeor Beach.*
3. *Most of the rocks are hidden __________ the surface.*

Debby is talking about how great it is that their parents left them alone and that she wished her father would do the same.

Linda keeps back a smile. Debby would take the chance to try and get a date with Josh, that's for sure. But she is glad that Debby is so concentrated on her subject that she doesn't realise how excited Linda is about meeting Cooper in an hour.

Again they meet Josh in the entrance of the gallery. It seems to be his task[5] to come and welcome the kids. Maybe this is necessary to get them past the cashier[6].

Linda is surprised how naturally he interacts with Jamie. Her brother is convinced that his putting bones together is an artistic act, and Josh supports this view of Jamie's tic[7].

But today he goes even further.

Exercise 74

Hauptsache: Unterstreiche die Substantive (keine Namen!) im vorigen Absatz und setze sie in den Plural oder Singular.

5 task – Aufgabe 6 cashier – Kassierer(in) 7 tic – Macke

"I've brought us some chlorine cleaner[8]. I'll show you how to use it. It turns the bones into snow white pieces of art. And if we cover them with a special colourless finish[9] they'll last forever. And we can put your sculptures in our 2012 Kids' Summer Expo. What do you think?"

Jamie nods fiercely, his face glowing with pride[10] like a light bulb. Linda is happy for him and for herself.

8 chlorine cleaner – Chlorreiniger 9 finish – Lack 10 pride – Stolz

Chapter 23

The clouds are still lingering over the graveyard, when Linda hurries up the steep hill to the top of the island, where Cooper should be in a few minutes. As she crosses the beach, Angus, the lighthouse keeper with the handbag face waves at her.

Exercise 75

Besserwisser: Welche der folgenden Aussagen ist falsch?

1. *Their parents leave Jamie and Linda alone.*
2. *Debby is keen on meeting the lighthouse keeper.*
3. *Josh in very friendly with Jamie.*

"Where's your brother? I've got something for him," he shouts and points into his boat. Even at this distance Linda can see the scar on his face. He looks a bit scary[1] to her.

"At the Tate. See you later!" Linda shouts back although she is not sure whether she should have said this.

At the top of the island a small chapel built out of natural stone keeps watch over St Ives and the sea. As Linda arrives the sign at the side of the chapel catches her attention.

"St Nicholas Chapel", that's where the name of their apartment block comes from, St Nicholas Court!

1 scary – beängstigend

Linda looks around, but Cooper is not there yet, only some tourists are standing on the slope[2] that points to the right hand side, where the smaller Porthgwidden Beach is, where they saw seals the day before. They are flying kites[3].

Exercise 76

Lückenfüller: Ergänze das fehlende Wort!

1. *The Mermaid Chair is situated in the ________________ of Zennor.*
2. *The Tate Gallery has a cafe on the ________________*
3. *Portmeor Beach is loved by ________________*

Some other tourists are on their way to the old watch station to take a look at what the coastguard used to do when the place was still used.

Linda turns back to the sign. It says St Nicholas is the patron saint of children and of sailors and the chapel was dated back further than 1434, when the town church was built. She bets even her father doesn't know that.

Linda sits down on the steps in front of the chapel. Her heart is beating against her ribs as she watches Cooper crossing the car park and heading towards her. She would like to run to him, throw herself into his arms, feel him. But she stays seated. She forces herself to look cool, calm and collected[4].

2 slope – Abhang 3 to fly kites – Drachen steigen lassen 4 cool, calm and collected – ruhig und gefasst

When Cooper stands in front of her with a vague and somehow unsettled[5] expression on his face she pulls him down by her side onto the steps.

Exercise 77

Strippenzieher: Verbinde die folgenden *phrasal verbs* (Verb mit Partikel) mit der richtigen deutschen Übersetzung.

keep at sthg.	*sich aus etw. heraushalten*
keep off	*etw. anbehalten*
keep it on	*weitermachen mit etw.*
keep out	*nicht betreten*

Cooper looks into her eyes, then puts his arms around her. It takes only seconds for Linda to relax.

"Here we are," Cooper says and kisses Linda's cheek.

"Why couldn't you wait? As agreed[6]?" Linda frees herself from his hug[7] and puts some space between them.

"What's wrong? I was missing you so much. And your parents have left. So what?"

"But we had agreed that you would wait until I told you you could come!"

"And if I had done so I would have arrived by tomorrow night, together with your parents. That wouldn't have made much sense, would it?"

5 unsettled – verunsichert 6 to agree – vereinbaren 7 hug – Umarmung

Exercise 78

Lückenfüller: Häng das passende Frageanhängsel (*question tag*, z. B. *You haven't seen her, have you?*) an.

1. *Linda has to wait for Cooper, ________________?*
2. *Cooper doesn't want to talk about his reasons for coming, ________________?*
3. *Jamie wants to build a chicken skeleton, ________________?*

"Oh, Cooper," is all Linda can say. In fact she is happy to see him and it is no use complaining. He is right, this solution is just perfect. So she takes his hand and pulls him behind the chapel.

She doesn't want Paul Bannister to see them. That man is always running around town, you never know where he will show up next.

In the safe shade at the back of the chapel they stand close, holding each other. Linda's head feels light as a balloon[8], and Cooper's kisses taste like candy floss[9]. They don't have to talk much. It feels as if time has stopped.
When the clock of the town church chimes two o'clock Linda is totally caught by surprise[10].

"I have to hurry, to pick up Jamie. I'll call you if I can bring him back to the gallery later. Okay?"

Cooper nods. One last kiss and Linda rushes off.

8 balloon – Luftballon 9 candy floss – Zuckerwatte 10 to be caught by surprise – überrascht werden

Exercise 79

Just do it: Unterstreiche die Verben auf Seite 98 im Absatz *In the safe shade* bis *has stopped* und konjugiere sie durch.

Chapter 24

The paved[1] slip road[2] to the garage almost disappears behind a fine veil[3] of light rain, but the yellow and blue squares on the sides of the two police cars can clearly be distinguished[4] from the front door.

Ruby remains in the background, while her parents are waiting for the police officers. She is surprised that two cars are necessary to take down the complaint[5].

Her father greets the two uniformed police officers and steps aside to let them in[6]. One is a man, Special Constable Rogers, who is about 50, with very short hair, so thick that it looks like grey fur[7] over a round face with friendly green eyes.

Exercise 80

Was wäre, wenn: Ergänze die fehlenden Verbformen in den folgenden If-Sätzen (Typ 1).

1. *If Linda is late, Josh (is) ________________ angry.*
2. *If Jamie gets glue, he (build) ________________ the skeleton.*
3. *If Debby gets money, she (buy) ________________ a new scarf.*

The second is a lady of about 30. She introduces herself as Crime Scene Specialist Hillary. Her face is triangular[8], her skin of a

1 paved – gepflastert 2 slip road – Einfahrt 3 veil – Schleier 4 to distinguish – erkennen, unterscheiden 5 complaint – Anzeige 6 to let in – hereinlassen 7 fur – Fell 8 triangular – dreieckig

remarkable dark olive with almond shaped[9] black eyes. She only reaches up to Ruby's nose and her body reminds her of a small school girl. Her truncheon[10] dangles from her hip like a third arm, and as she moves, it hits her knee.

They walk into the living room. Ruby would like to join them to find out if somebody suspects Cooper, but her father sends her into the kitchen to make some coffee.

When she returns to the living room and puts the tray with the cups down on the coffee table, Constable Rogers is just saying, "Well, lately some gangs of car thieves[11] from the Continent have been active around Oxford and in North London. They usually stay only one night in an area, break up all kinds of new and valuable cars, and store them in villages for several days until they have changed the colour and number plates."

Exercise 81

„Am Lesen sein“: Setze die folgenden Verben in die Verlaufsform.

1. *Ruby (stay) ________________ in the background.*
2. *They (walk) ________________ into the living room.*
3. *They (put) ________________ their notebooks on the table.*

"Gosh, my car was only three weeks old! It's a German SUV! I want it back! What are you going to do to find it?"

"We'll give out a detailed request to all police stations in the

9 almond shaped – mandelförmig 10 truncheor – Schlagstock 11 car thief – Autoknacker

county and to the Ferry Companies at the Channel. And we'll start a local search with our forces."

"And if that doesn't lead anywhere?"

"Good question. Then we ..."

Specialist Hillary, who was absent then, as Ruby only realises now, steps in from the terrace. Her uniform is wet with rain and so is her black ponytail[12]. She sits down beside her colleague and takes one of the coffee cups.

"Thank you. That's good. Are you sure the garage was properly closed? There is not a single sign of a break-in[13]," she asks in Ruby's father's direction.

"We were on holiday, as I've told you already. But the garage is always only pushed shut. We don't usually lock it up[14]. As you have seen the estate is circled by a wall and a gate, so it should be safe that way."

He looks at Ruby. "The door was closed, wasn't it?"

"Sure. As I told you, we haven't used the bikes for the last four days. So nobody needed to go into the garage."

Exercise 82

Wessen? Setze die folgenden Begriffe in den Genitiv.

1. *the police officers + notebooks* ____________________
2. *Ruby + parents + kitchen* ____________________
3. *boss + disappearance* ____________________

12 ponytail – Pferdeschwanz 13 break-in – Einbruch 14 to lock up – abschließen

Ruby looks at her feet. She wishes she was as positive inside as she appears on the outside.

"Okay then," Detective Hillary sums up, "we'll check the surroundings and see what we can find out. If we don't succeed[15] with this strategy we will put it in the local paper. These gangs have specialised in tourist cars. They usually don't break into garages. Maybe somebody has seen something …"

15 succeed – Erfolg haben

Chapter 25

"Look, how shiny they are now!"

Jamie proudly presents the whitened bones to Linda.

They are sitting at their kitchen table.

Linda can't get over Josh's reaction when she came to get her brother. Josh had been really angry when she was late. Everybody else from the course had left and the two were sitting in front of the gallery. When Linda asked when Jamie could come back, Josh said, „I have a training course[1], so no invitation this afternoon, I'm sorry". But she had only been ten minutes late.

Linda is not sure whether Jamie has understood that he can't go back to see Josh this afternoon. He is so happy with the bleached bones that he can't stop rearranging them over and over again, like shuffling[2] a deck of cards[3].

She herself is as disappointed as she thinks Debby must be, for different reasons. Cooper will have to wait until tonight. She has already texted him that. His mobile is switched off, just in case his parents try to call him. Linda is quite unhappy because she remembers Ruby telling her that their parents think Cooper is in Scotland. But she is not a bit better herself. She would lie to her parents, too, if they asked her about Cooper.

Now she only hopes Cooper will understand that she can't leave her brother alone, even if his mood is great at the moment. That can change within seconds.

1 training course – Weiterbildung 2 to shuffle – mischen 3 deck of cards – Kartenspiel

Exercise 83

Parallelwelten: Finde die Gegenteilpaare und verbinde sie mit Strichen.

dirty	*short*
question	*ceiling*
wet	*clean*
floor	*answer*
long	*dry*

"Come on, Jamie," she suggests as she finishes cleaning the dishes of the reminders of grilled cheese sandwiches and ready made cucumber salad and puts them into the dishwasher.

"Let's see if we can watch the fisherman at the beach. Maybe he has made a big catch for you."

On their way down the stairs they bump into Paul Bannister and Debby.

"Hi there. What are you two doing now?" he asks.

"Going to the beach to watch the fisherman and the birds," Linda replies.

"Great. And Jamie, if you like, we can work on something tomorrow. I have some nice tools I would like to show to you."

Jamie doesn't look too enthusiastic, but he nods.

"Well, have fun. We have bought some painting stuff for Debby and want to try it out."

Debby lifts an expensive[4] looking wooden case with small tubes of oil paint and a packet of different sized brushes. Her father is carrying two table sized pieces of framed canvas. Obviously he has to take over the artistic part of Josh's job.

Linda nods her head. She doesn't like this man, that's for sure. He is trying too hard to be everybody's closest friend.

Exercise 84

Viele: Bilde den Plural der folgenden Substantive.

1. *patch* ____________________
2. *half* ____________________
3. *fish* ____________________
4. *mouth* ____________________
5. *bus* ____________________

At the beach it is low tide. The surfers are leaving as the waves are pretty small now and the rocks are showing at the surface again.

But the good thing about low tide is, that Angus, the lighthouse keeper, is back with his boat. It is lying on one side like a dead whale. And he is smiling his scary half smile as he recognises Jamie.

"Come here, boy, I've got something for you!"

Another dead fish, Linda thinks and prepares herself for an ugly impression. But when she can see what is hidden in the boat

4 expensive – kostspielig

she has to turn and swallow. She grabs for Jamie's hand, but her brother is not such as wimp[5] as she is. When Linda is sure she can take another look without vomiting[6], she watches her little brother stroking the dead seal.

Exercise 85

Satzsalat: Bringe die Wörter in die richtige Reihenfolge!

1. *a better herself bit is Linda not.*

   ____

2. *the has fisher for a big maybe catch you.*

   ____

3. *already it tide is low.*

   ____

"Can we get the bones out of him?" Jamie asks and Linda would like to sink into the earth[7]. But Angus does not hesitate to reply as if Jamie's question was the most usual request, "Of course we can, we only need a big Bunsen burner[8]. Do you know where we can find one?"

All of a sudden Jamie starts screaming. He runs behind Linda and puts her arms around him, crying „Bolt! Bolt! Bolt!"

Linda is absolutely surprised by his reaction. A second before this outburst Jamie seemed so fond of the plan of getting the seal's bones, and now this.

5 wimp – *ugs.:* Weichei 6 to vomit – sich übergeben, brechen 7 to sink into the earth – im Erdboden versinken 8 Bunsen burner – Bunsenbrenner

Exercise 86

Besserwisser: Steigere die folgenden Adjektive.

1. *little (wenig),* ____________________, ____________________
2. *little (klein),* ____________________, ____________________
3. *many,* ____________________, ____________________
4. *much,* ____________________, ____________________

She pulls her brother towards the house, away from Angus, away from the beach and this dead seal. The fisherman looks puzzled, too. But he doesn't ask what is wrong.

Perhaps he knows how strange the plan to burn the flesh off the dead seal is.

Chapter 26

Late that night, when Jamie had calmed down with the help of a counting game and his chicken bones, when he is in his bed and fast asleep, Linda lets Cooper into the apartment.

First she steps outside the door and makes sure the lights next door in the Bannisters' rooms are switched off. Then she sneaks[1] down the open staircase, through the covered passage to the street. Nobody is to be seen, she is on her own in the darkness.

Cooper is waiting in a doorway on the opposite side of the road. When Linda waves at him, he follows her hastily[2] up the stairs, into the apartment and into her room.

"Puh," Linda gasps[3], "that was lucky."

Cooper pulls her into his arms and she feels her tension fall from her neck muscles. She is so glad that he is with her now.

"I have to go back to the Backpacker's early tomorrow morning," Cooper says when they take a break to breathe, "my money was stolen last night or I lost it, I don't know. I couldn't pay for the night, so they want me to work for it."

"Oh no, that's too bad! How are you going to get back home? And what are you going to do when my parents are back? You can sleep here tonight, but not when they are here."

"I know," Cooper says, "I think I can work there for a while. But that means, we can't meet much …"

"Great," Linda tries to stop being sarcastic, but her heart is aching.

1 to sneak – schleichen 2 hastily – fluchtartig, rasch 3 to gasp – schnaufen

Exercise 87

Wortverdreher: Bilde Fragen aus den folgenden Sätzen, indem du die Wortstellung veränderst und Wörter ergänzt, wo nötig.

1. *Angus calls Jamie.*

   ____

2. *Jamie strokes the dead seal.*

   ____

3. *Linda takes Jamie home.*

   ____

"Let's use the time we have." Cooper strokes her cheek with his soft lips and puts his arm around her shoulders.

Linda avoids thinking about the next days and leans back, but the happiness and joy she had felt about seeing Cooper are gone and won't come back. After a while Linda gently pushes him away and gets up.

"Don't take liberties[4]," she says in the tone of an old fashioned lady and waves her index finger in front of Cooper's face. "You can't sleep here."

Cooper shows his disappointment, but he follows her into the living room. As they pass Jamie's door, Linda signals Cooper to watch his steps in order not to wake him up.

4 to take liberties – sich Freiheiten herausnehmen

Exercise 88

Zeitreise: Setze die Verben in die Zukunftsform (*future*, z. B. *will go*).

1. *Jamie (goes) ________________ to bed.*
2. *Linda (invites) ________________ Cooper into the apartment.*
3. *He (follows) ________________ her up the stairs.*
4. *Cooper (works) ________________ for the Backpacker's.*

The next morning Linda wakes up at eight and rushes to the living room to make Cooper leave before Jamie gets up and discovers him. Cooper is sleeping like a log[5] and turns around twice. Only when she uses a wet towel on his face does he sit up.

Linda almost has to push him out of the door after a short look around.

"Go to work, young man, and call me when you have the time." Linda kisses Cooper goodbye and walks to Jamie's room.

She opens the door silently and all at once her blood freezes. She steps to the side of her brother's bed. But she does not have to pull the duvet back to realise what is obvious:

Jamie's bed is deserted[6] and the chair where they had put his clothes last night is empty.

Linda runs to the bathroom, she pulls the shower curtain aside. Then she rushes back into Jamie's room.

5 to sleep like a log – wie ein Murmeltier schlafer 6 deserted – verlassen

"Jamie, be a good boy! Come out"! Linda opens the doors of the wooden wardrobe. It is full of blue clothes. She pushes the hanging garments aside, leans forward to examine every corner. But it is empty.

Jamie is gone!

Chapter 27

6,785, 6,786, 6,787, 6,788, 6,789, 6,790, 6,791, …

Hmmhmmm …

It is okay. Nothing bad has happened.

6,792, 6,793, 6,794, …

Hmmm, hmmm …

It is not dangerous. This is different. You can see them. No hidden dangers …

Exercise 89

Buchstabensalat: Sortiere die Buchstaben so, dass sinnvolle Wörter entstehen!

1. *nnghiot* ____________________
2. *itinvonati* ____________________
3. *ushtohlige* ____________________

6,795, 6,796, 6,797, 6,798, 6,799, 6,800, 6,801 …

Hmm, hmmm …

The faces in your book won't help this time. This expression is not in your book. What does Doc Wiseguy say? Look for an expression that comes close to what you see …

6,802, 6,803, 6,804, 6,805 ….

Exercise 90

Besserwisser: Welche der folgenden Aussagen ist falsch?

1. *Jamie freaked out at the beach.*
2. *Angus showed a dead seal to Jamie.*
3. *Paul Bannister tried to beat Jamie.*

Hmmm, hmmm …

You saw a smile like that on page 5. Didn't you? Was it a smile? Are you sure?

Bolt, bolt? Bolt?

6,806, 6,807 …

But there is the promise, and the new tool. Everything will even be nicer than last time. And he can be trusted, he is a good guy …

Hmmm, hmmm ….

Chapter 28

"Come on Hamlet!"

Special Constable Rogers leans over the counter in Bath police station and has to swallow a laugh.

This Hamlet is definitely not the Prince of Denmark. This Hamlet is a dog that looks like a pig with the spotted fur of a black and white milk cow. He moves like a steamship in a storm, bouncing[1] heavily from one side to the other. And he sounds like a steamer, too.

Exercise 91

Verbbeuger: Ergänze die fehlenden Konjugationsformen der folgenden Verben (z. B. *go, went, gone*).

1. ____________________, *beat, beaten*
2. ____________________, *began, begun*
3. ____________________, *chose, chosen*

Hamlet is accompanied by an elderly couple in long rain coats with rain hats on, although the sun is out.

"We have read the newspaper, the request[2] about a missing car."

"The German SUV that is missing?"

1 to bounce – wackeln 2 request – Anfrage

"Exactly." The man rubs his nose. "We saw it. A young bloke[3] was behind the wheel, driving like hell, he hit the footpath and some rubbish containers."

Exercise 92

Lückenfüller: Häng das passende Frageanhängsel (*question tag*, z. B. *You haven't seen her, have you?*) an.

1. *Hamlet looks like a pig, ________________?*
2. *The old man rubs his nose, ________________?*
3. *The Detective is not busy, ________________?*

"When and where exactly did this happen? And can you describe the man?" Rogers is taking notes.

"Richard did not see the number plate, his eyesight …" the old lady says in a regretful[4] tone.

"Oh Heather, stop it! The car was too fast! You didn't either!"

"Don't worry. The other details will be enough, I hope," the Constable replies with a smile and calls Special Constable Hillary for assistance.

Two hours later Ruby crumples[5] a paper towel in her hands and examines the remainder in her lap.

The two police officers have just pointed out[6] how they found the car. It was severely damaged. Everything looked as if

3 bloke – Bursche, Kerl 4 regretful – bedauernd 5 to crumple – zerknittern 6 to point out – darlegen

somebody had stolen it, had an accident and hid the broken car in a nearby wood.

Exercise 93

„Am Lesen sein": Setze die folgenden Verben in die Verlaufsform.

1. *A young guy (drove) ________________ the car.*
2. *The music (hammered) ________________ out of the radio.*
3. *The car (sped) ________________ through the village.*

"Everything indicates[7] an inexperienced driver," the Crime Scene Specialist says. Ruby feels everybody's eyes burning holes into her forehead. She doesn't dare to look up.

"You see, professional burglars, especially gangs, always act quickly and without attracting attention. But this tour was quite spectacular. A young driver with the radio turned up and driving at high speed …"

Ruby's father clears his throat[8]. "So Ruby, is there anything you want to tell us? Anything connected with Cooper?"

Ruby softly shakes her head, but when nobody says a word she finally looks up and tells the whole story, about the party, about her getting a bit tipsy[9].

"You mean drunk!" her mother exclaims.

And about Cooper taking somebody home.

"Who was it? We have to call them. Maybe somebody is hurt."

7 to indicate – hindeuten 8 to clear o.'s throat – sich räuspern 9 tipsy – beschwipst

Ruby just shakes her head. She doesn't want Melinda to get involved.

Exercise 94

Strippenzieher: Verbinde die folgenden *phrasal verbs* (Verb mit Partikel) mit der richtigen deutschen Übersetzung.

make off	*zur Seite legen*
make out	*erkennen*
put across	*sich davon machen*
put aside	*vermitteln*

And she doesn't mention her vision of Jamie in the car. Hopefully this was just her imagination. Otherwise her poor brother would have a lot more to explain …

Chapter 29

Linda is completely out of breath. Jamie is not at the art course at the Tate. Josh and Debby were both concerned and offered to help them look for Jamie, but Linda had turned it down. She first wanted to talk to Cooper. Maybe he had heard something last night.

Linda pushes herself forward through the tourists in Fore Street, the busiest shopping street in St Ives. She turns right at the church and hurries up the shortest way to the Backpacker's.

Exercise 95

Just do it: Unterstreiche die Verben im vorigen Absatz und konjugiere sie durch.

____

____

The third person, judging by his age the warden[1], whom Linda asks at the hostel, knows Cooper.

"He slept here two nights ago, left his backpack yesterday and popped up[2] this morning to get his stuff. I think he moved on[3]."

Linda's hands get ice cold and goose pimples[4] run down her back.

"Did he pay all right?"

"Yep. No worries. Everything is settled."

1 warden – Herbergsvater 2 to pop up – auftauchen 3 to move on – weiterziehen 4 goose pimples – Gänsehaut

Exercise 96

Wessen? Setze die folgenden Begriffe in den Genitiv.

1. *Angus + lighthouse* ______________________
2. *Josh + art course* ______________________
3. *the shops + closing time* ______________________

Linda runs back to the harbour, hoping that Jamie might be with Angus, counting the loops[5] of the net or the seagulls. Those big birds like the harbour walk, because they can steal fish and chips from the numerous tourists who are having their lunch there. But the lighthouse keeper must be out with his boat, and Jamie is not there either.

Linda lets herself drop on one of the benches and swallows on a big lump in her throat.

Exercise 97

Zeitreise: Setze die Verben in die einfache Vergangenheit (*past tense*, z. B. *went*).

1. *Debby (bite)* ______________ *into her scone.*
2. *Josh (draws)* ______________ *a picture.*
3. *Linda (digs)* ______________ *out a seashell.*

5 loop – Masche

What shall I do? Call Mum and Dad? Go to Paul Bannister? But that man is suspicious himself. And if Jamie was there Debby would have told her.

Finally she calls Ruby.

"That can't be true!" Linda cries out after Ruby has told her what the police have found out and what their parents reconstructed.

"He stole your Dad's car and had an accident? And hid it to make it look like a theft[6]? Are you sure it was Cooper?"

Ruby sounds weak, she is sobbing from time to time and Linda can imagine how she must feel. She feels sick herself, sick from fear about Jamie and from anger about Cooper.

Ruby goes on. „They found his baseball cap, we are positive[7]. And we can't reach him. This is really bad for Cooper. And it is getting worse[8] the longer he doesn't show up[9]. And I'm not sure …" Ruby pauses. "But I think I saw Jamie in the car shortly before Cooper took it …"

Exercise 98

Viele: Bilde den Plural der folgenden Substantive!

1. *sandwich* ____________________
2. *bush* ____________________
3. *family* ____________________
4. *day* ____________________

6 theft – Diebstahl 7 positive – *hier:* sicher 8 worse – schlimmer 9 to show up – aufkreuzen

Linda's stomach turns and her blood knocks against her ears from the inside. She is unable to say a word, paralysed by the image that comes to her like a photograph.

The bruise on Jamie's belly she had seen the day after the party, it is clear like a photo. And when Jamie undressed last night she saw that it was not only on his belly but reached over his chest up to his shoulder. Exactly where the safety belt would stop a kid from smashing into the front window in a car crash. Not as black as it was two days ago, but still green.

"I have to find Cooper," she whispers and puts her mobile away.

Chapter 30

"This would be a nice hiding place if one had to hide," Cooper had said the day before as they were sitting in front of St Nicholas Chapel on the island.

Exercise 99

Satzsalat: Bringe die Wörter in die richtige Reihenfolge!

1. *back to Linda harbour the runs.*

   ____

2. *be true can't that.*

   ____

3. *in saw I the Jamie car.*

   ____

Linda rushes up the hill, passing people with kites.

From the distance she can see that nobody is near the chapel. But maybe Cooper is inside. Maybe he kidnapped Jamie the night before and hid him in the chapel so Jamie can't reveal[1] Cooper's secret about the theft and the accident. And Cooper came back to cover his tracks[2].

1 to reveal – verraten 2 to cover the tracks – die Spuren verwischen

Linda throws herself against the heavy wooden door, but it is locked. She hammers with her fists against the door, but nothing happens.

"Cooper, are you in there? Open the door, I know what you have done! Open it right now!"

She steps back. Nothing happens. Then she sees the sign on the doors:

"Open to the public from 10 to 12."

Exercise 100

Wortverdreher: Bilde Fragen aus den folgenden Sätzen, indem du die Wortstellung veränderst und Wörter ergänzt, wo nötig.

1. *Linda rushes up the hill.*

   ____

2. *Linda throws herself against the door.*

   ____

3. *She sees the sign.*

   ____

She hesitates for a moment, figuring out what time it is. Around midday. Their parents will be back in a few hours.

Linda knocks again. And this time she has the impression

that somebody inside is reacting. After another minute she hears something heavy being moved behind the door.

And Cooper comes out. His face is grey. But when Linda steps inside the chapel she sees that Cooper is all alone.

As she looks around she can't find a single trace of her little brother.

Chapter 31

"What did you do to Jamie?", she cries and beats against Cooper's breast.

"So you know what happened?"

"Yes, the police are after you. But where is my little brother?"

Cooper holds her fists firmly and looks into Linda's eyes. "I made a horrible mistake with my Dad's car. That's true. And I lied and tried to get away with it. But I didn't do anything to Jamie. He just ran away after the crash. And as you didn't mention him, I was sure he was fine."

A couple of tourists in colourful rain gear walk by and look at them. "Everything okay with you two?" A woman asks and looks at Linda.

Cooper releases her arms at once.

"Yes, we are fine. Thank you," Linda replies and takes Cooper's hand.

"We have to talk to Paul Bannister. Although I don't like that man. And call my parents. I hope Jamie is fine …"

She drags Cooper down the hill towards their apartment block, but Cooper hesitates.

"Stop this, Cooper. Why didn't you tell me about the accident before? You have to admit what you have done. Your parents will forgive you. My Dad always says 'it's only things. Things can be replaced'."

"It is not that easy to replace an expensive SUV as this, believe me. And my father will not pay for my driving licence any more. I bet there will be no driving licence at all."

Exercise 101

Buchstabensalat: Sortiere die Buchstaben so, dass sinnvolle Wörter entstehen!

1. *pidnaknpig* ______________________
2. *ulorfculo* ______________________
3. *enclice* ______________________

Paul Bannister opens at once as if he had been waiting for them. Debby stands beside him and watches Cooper like a snake.

After Linda explained all the circumstances of Cooper's appearance in St Ives, about the car theft and Jamie's disappearance, Paul Bannister questions her about every detail from the last day and night. He hesitates when Linda tells him about the dead seal and Angus' suggestion to put it on the Bunsen burner. He frowns[1] at the point when Jamie freaked out at the beach, and Cooper interrupts her.

"That was when he saw me. I was at the far end of the beach, waiting for you, Linda, and Jamie recognised me. I think he remembered the accident ..."

Linda's mouth drops open and Bannister shakes his head.

"Okay, I can only think of one place where Jamie could be: At Angus' place, at the lighthouse. Let's go there."

1 to frown – die Stirn runzeln

"But that's impossible," Linda utters. She feels a fist closing around her stomach. "Jamie is afraid of rays, this is why he always switches his mobile phone off."

"Well, maybe the idea of getting a whole seal skeleton was stronger than his fear."

Chapter 32

As they approach the pier with the lighthouse at the end, the waves are beating against the stone walls, bringing in the fishermen's boats. Angus is among them. He waves both arms to them and Linda waves back.

As she looks at Paul Bannister she can't tell what he is thinking. She is not sure, what the expression means: fear? Doubt? Anger? Or just curiosity?

Angus attaches his boat to the pier and climbs up the iron ladder. He leaves the boxes with his catch behind and wipes his forearm over his face.

"There you are. I've been expecting you. I tried to call you, but I left my mobile at the lighthouse when I went fishing early this morning. Realised it only when I was far out at the fishing grounds. But I see you figured out where he is, your little brother. Came here at night. Because of a guy with a car, who said he would beat him if he told anyone. That's you, huh?" He points his potato nose towards Cooper.

"You threatened Jamie?" Linda exclaims and turns away, towards the doors. "Go away, Cooper, stay away from me, from him." She turns to Bannister: "Wait here!" And towards Angus: "Can we look after him now?"

"Of course."

Angus opens the door, Linda follows him up the spiral stairs. At the top there is a small room. Jamie is sitting at a round table, watching the light of the tower turn around again and again. Linda can see his lips moving.

Jamie looks happy. He is counting rays.

Final Quiz

1. *Where do Linda and her family live and where do they travel to for their summer holiday?*

2. *Why is it so difficult for Linda to find out what Cooper is doing?*

3. *What is strange about Jamie when the family wants to leave the petrol station after the break?*

4. *Why is Ruby so angry about her brother right at the beginning?*

5. *What is the very first hint for Linda that Cooper has not kept to what they agreed before she left?*

6. *What makes Cooper leave earlier for Cornwall than he had agreed with Linda?*

____

____

7. *Why is Linda not willing to take part in the art course at the Tate Gallery?*

____

____

8. *Why does Linda distrust Paul Bannister?*

____

____

9. *Why does Jamie like Josh Burns so very much?*

____

____

10. *What does Jamie fear most?*

____

____

Answer key to the Exercises

Exercise 1:	1. the car's number plate, 2. the man's hat, 3. the woman's dog
Exercise 2:	1. barks, 2. frowns, 3. shakes
Exercise 3:	loud – silent, dark – bright, fat – slim, day – night, hot – cold
Exercise 4:	1. felt, 2. shook, 3. was
Exercise 5:	1. women, 2. dogs, 3. men, 4. children, houses
Exercise 6:	1. loud, 2. quickly, 3. carefully
Exercise 7:	1. Rattler is a strong cider. 2. Cooper must have accompanied her home. 3. Jamie has been deep asleep since they got on the motorway.
Exercise 8:	1. has fallen, 2. has been, 3. have been
Exercise 9:	1, louder, loudest, 2. better, best, 3. shorter, shortest, 4. more careful, most careful, 5. nicer, nicest
Exercise 10:	1. Does Jamie count everything? 2. Does Linda want to be with Cooper? 3. Is their mother suggesting solutions?
Exercise 11:	1. will collect, 2. will look, 3. will send
Exercise 12:	1. engine, 2. somebody, 3. toilet
Exercise 13:	1. about, 2. into, 3. into
Exercise 14:	cardboard – cardboard, faces – face, gestures – gesture, figure – figures, hand – hands, index finger – index fingers, teacher – teachers, gesture – gestures, kid – kids

Exercise 15:	to go off – explodieren, to go for – anstreben, to look for – suchen, to look forward to – sich freuen auf
Exercise 16:	1
Exercise 17:	1. rubbish, 2. stomach ache, 3. appearance
Exercise 18:	1. heard, heard, 2. looked, looked, 3. saw, seen
Exercise 19:	1. Obviously he had a few beers too many last night. 2. She hears herself again calling Jamie last night. 3. Ruby decides not to ask Cooper about Melinda.
Exercise 20:	1. didn't she? 2. has she? 3. didn't he?
Exercise 21:	remember, remembered, remembered; see, saw, seen; sit, sat, sat; prance, pranced, pranced; wait, waited, waited; watch, watched, watched
Exercise 22:	1. will go, 2. will call, 3. will go
Exercise 23:	1. is counting, 2. is reading, 3. is driving
Exercise 24:	1. is going to call, 2. is going to lock, 3. is going to cook
Exercise 25:	1. would feel, 2. would eat, 3. would get
Exercise 26:	1. Jamie is able to count. 2. Linda is not allowed to use her phone. 3. Linda is not allowed to text either.
Exercise 27:	1. must/have to, 2. must/has to, 3. must/has to
Exercise 28:	1. You don't have to eat that. 2.Linda doesn't have to put her mobile phone away. 3. Their father does not have to lock the door.
Exercise 29:	1. Linda must/may not use her mobile. 2. Jamie must/may not go out on his own. 3. Their parents must/may not quarrel.

Exercise 30: 1. Their parents would accept his running away. 2. And why does she feel so bad about him leaving? 3. Ruby watches Cooper turn pale.

Exercise 31: 1. Ruby's vision, 2. Their parents' house, 3. Ruby and Cooper's parents

Exercise 32: 1. hears, 2. drives, 3. come

Exercise 33: forward – backward, right – left, correct – wrong, right – wrong, hard – soft, weak – strong

Exercise 34: 1. wore, 2. ate, 3. went

Exercise 35: geese, mice, lice

Exercise 36: 1. hastily, 2. bright, 3. irregularly

Exercise 37: 1. Jamie seems to like Debby and her father. 2. Where can Jamie be? 3. He must be counting the wipes again.

Exercise 38: 1. has turned, 2. have quarrelled, 3. have talked

Exercise 39: 1. more different, most different, 2. prouder, proudest, 3. more handsome, most handsome

Exercise 40: 1. Is Linda used to this gesture? 2. Does Josh look quite handsome? 3. Does Debby seem to be proud of the teacher?

Exercise 41: 1. will follow, 2. will talk, 3. will show

Exercise 42: 1. exhibition, 2. painting, 3. limestone

Exercise 43: 1. You must/may not leave Jamie alone. 2. Jamie must/may not play with dead animals. 3. Debby must/may not flirt with Josh.

Exercise 44: 1. on, at; 2. from, from, from; 3. at

Exercise 45: 2

Exercise 46: voice – voices, café – cafés, roof – roofs, Gallery – Galleries, mobile phone – mobile phones

Exercise 47:	1. still life, limestone, waitress
Exercise 48:	1. take, taken; 2. caught, caught, 3. stand, stood
Exercise 49:	call for – verlangen, call off – absagen, carry on – weitermachen, carry out – ausführen
Exercise 50:	1. isn't she? 2. doesn't she? 3. was she?
Exercise 51:	think, thought, thought; happen, happened, happened; mean, meant, meant; know, knew, known
Exercise 52:	1. tells, 2. tells, 3. will have
Exercise 53:	1. is rising, 2. are surfing, 3. are complaining
Exercise 54:	1. are going to dive, 2. is going to leave, 3. is going to walk
Exercise 55:	1. would walk, 2. would admire, 3. would argue
Exercise 56:	1. Are the kids allowed to complain? 2. Is Jamie allowed to walk to the Tate on his own? 3. Is Linda able to carry her little brother?
Exercise 57:	1. Must you/Do you have to be so loud? 2. You must/You have to be here before 10 o'clock! 3. You must not lie to your parents!
Exercise 58:	1. You don't have to eat it up. 2. You don't have to read that book. 3. We don't have to walk to Zennor.
Exercise 59:	1. They must/may not go to the beach at night. 2. We must/may not leave the doors unlocked. 3. I must/may not be late.
Exercise 60:	1. Of course, they all have seen the cushion, they are not blind! 2. You have to know the history of this symbol. 3. But one night she couldn't stand her longing for his voice any longer.

Exercise 61: 1. the Mermaid's Chair, 2. the students' courses, 3. the horse's saddle

Exercise 62: 1. comes, 2. listens, 3. vanishes

Exercise 63: open – close, left – right, above – under, in front – behind, naked – dressed

Exercise 64: 1. took, dragged; 2. left, 3. shook

Exercise 65: 1. buses (im amerikanischen Englisch: busses), 2. policemen, 3. galleries

Exercise 66: 1. wonderfully, 2. horrible, 3. freshly

Exercise 67: 1. They all go into the supermarket. 2. Jamie needs the bones for the art class. 3. Her father gets loud every once in a while.

Exercise 68: 1. has taken, 2. has been fed up, 3. has tried

Exercise 69: 1, larger, largest; 2. bigger, biggest; 3. sunnier, sunniest

Exercise 70: 1. Is Linda fast asleep? 2. Does she hide under her duvet? 3. Are there more places her mother would like to visit?

Exercise 71: 1. will get, 2. will drink, 3. will travel

Exercise 72: 1. Wednesday, 2. opportunity, 3. enthusiasm

Exercise 73: 1. of, 2. along, 3. under

Exercise 74: brother – brothers, bones – bone, act – acts, view – views, tic – tics

Exercise 75: 2

Exercise 76: 1. church, 2. roof, 3. surfers

Exercise 77: keep at sth. – weitermachen mit etwas, keep off – nicht betreten, keep it on – etwas anbehalten, keep out – sich heraushalten aus

Exercise 78: 1. doesn't she? 2. does he? 3. doesn't he?

Exercise 79: stand, stood, stood; hold, held, held; feel, felt, felt; taste, tasted, tasted; talk, talked, talked; feel, felt, felt; stop, stopped, stopped

Exercise 80: 1. will be, 2. will build, 3. will buy

Exercise 81: 1. is keeping, 2. are walking, 3. are putting

Exercise 82: 1. the police officers' notebooks, 2. Ruby's parents' kitchen, 3. boss's disappearance

Exercise 83: dirty – clean, question – answer, wet – dry, floor – ceiling, long – short

Exercise 84: 1. patches, 2. halves, 3. fish, 4. mouths, 5. buses

Exercise 85: 1. Linda is not a bit better herself . 2. Maybe the fisherman has a big catch for you. 3. It is already low tide.

Exercise 86: 1. less, least; 2. smaller, smallest; 3. more, most (viele einzelne); 4. more, most (viel)

Exercise 87: 1. Does Angus call Jamie? 2. Does Jamie stroke the dead seal? 3. Does Linda take Jamie home?

Exercise 88: 1. will go, 2. will invite, 3. will follow, 4. will work

Exercise 89: 1. nothing, 2. invitation, 3. lighthouse

Exercise 90: 3.

Exercise 91: 1. beat, 2. begin, 3. choose

Exercise 92: 1. doesn't he? 2. doesn't he? 3. is he?

Exercise 93: 1. was driving, 2. was hammering, 3. was speeding

Exercise 94: make off – sich davon machen, make out – erkennen, put across – vermitteln, put by – zur Seite legen

Exercise 95: push, pushed, pushed; turn, turned, turned; hurry, hurried, hurried

Exercise 96: 1. Angus' lighthouse, 2. Josh's art course, 3. the shops' closing time

Exercise 97: 1. bit, 2. drew, 3. dug

Exercise 98: 1. sandwiches, bushes, families, days

Exercise 99: 1. Linda runs back to the harbour. 2. That can't be true. 3. I saw Jamie in the car.

Exercise 100: 1. Does Linda rush up the hill? 2. Does she throw herself against the door? 3. Does she see the sign?

Exercise 101: 1. kidnapping, 2. colourful, 3. licence

FINAL QUIZ: SOLUTIONS

1. Linda's family lives close to Bath. They travel to Cornwall for their summer holiday.
2. Linda is not allowed to use her mobile phone during their holiday.
3. Jamie has forgotten the time. He stays in the toilet, counting tiles, and freaks out because something we don't know has alarmed him.
4. Ruby thinks Cooper took Melinda home and betrayed Linda, her best friend.
5. When Linda talks to Cooper the first night she is in St Ives, he insists on coming to Cornwall right away.
6. Cooper leaves early because his parents come back from their holidays one day earlier than expected.
7. Linda needs the time when Jamie is under supervision in the arts course to make her phone calls.
8. Linda distrusts Paul Bannister because he is too friendly to everybody.
9. Jamie likes Josh Burns because he brings some bleach for the bones.
10. Jamie fears all kinds of rays, especially invisible ones.